BEAUDY

BEAUDY

Skills, drills & the path to the top

with Rikki Swannell

Acknowledgements
Rikki Swannell would like to thank Robyn Barrett, Phil Walter, Simon Hickey and Dean Hegan and the whole team at Halo Sport for their help and support during the writing of this book.

About the writer
Rikki Swannell has become a recognised face and voice in New Zealand sports broadcasting since the early 2000s. She is a commentator on domestic and international rugby, the World Sevens series, netball, tennis and other sports, and has worked as a reporter at several Olympic and Commonwealth Games.

A catalogue record for this book is available from the National Library of New Zealand

ISBN 978-1-99-000305-9

A Mower Book
Published in 2020 by Upstart Press Ltd
Level 6, BDO Tower, 19–21 Como St, Takapuna, Auckland 0622, New Zealand

Printed by Everbest Printing Co. Ltd., China

Designed by Nick Turzynski/Redinc. Book Design, www.redinc.co.nz
Cover photos: Getty Images

Dedication

To my mum and dad, for the endless opportunities and support. Thank you to my coaches who have all had an impact on my growth and development as a player and person; and to my teammates for fun and challenging times on and off the field. Lastly, to my beautiful wife Hannah for your unconditional love.

Contents

Foreword

Our kids were born into a life of sport. They never had flash toys; instead they had sports gear. Round balls, oval balls, bats, rackets, wickets and golf clubs — you name it, they were into it all, and Beauden was the ringleader when it came to organising a game.

He will always say he was just another player and nothing special as he came through the rugby grades, but that simply wasn't the case. People who watched him grow up and who have seen him play from a young age will tell you he was a gifted sportsman regardless of what code he was competing in and always stood out. He was never greedy and always a team player, but he did score a lot of tries when he was in the primary school teams.

Most importantly, though, he has always enjoyed his sport: the excitement that comes with competing and improving, having fun with his brothers and sisters, and his mates. That's what sport is all about. I have no doubt that the active, sporty and fun childhood Beauden had would have set him up for life regardless of whether he managed to make a career out of rugby.

Our family has been in Taranaki for generations. I was lucky enough to play more than 150 games for the province, so it's been a thrill to see my sons turn out for the Amber and Blacks. Mindful of having any undue influence because of my reputation in the area, I never coached any of the boys beyond primary school and everything Beauden and his brothers have achieved is purely on their own merits and because of the paths they paved for themselves. It is wonderful, though, to see how Beaudy's success is enjoyed by so many people in Taranaki, particularly the older generation, friends of my parents, who get a real buzz from having our region put up in lights.

When he was first playing for Taranaki and the Hurricanes, I would, more often than not, be a bundle of nerves. Robyn and I would be in the stands with our knees knocking together, unable to sit still as he lined up a kick at goal or if the ball was coming his way. As time has gone on and the nerves have calmed down a bit, I now get the same enjoyment seeing Beaudy play that many people do; he's so exciting to watch, gets the crowd on its feet and there's a sense of anticipation when he touches the ball.

We have always understood the importance of being fit and healthy, and I believe Beaudy's superior fitness, aerobic capacity and skill level are what sets him apart from other players. We've seen him do brilliant things towards halftime or at the end of games and that's no fluke or coincidence but rather because he often has extra in the tank and can pounce when others are tiring physically or hanging on for the whistle. Right from when he was a wee fella, Beaudy had determination that was next level.

Every parent hopes for the best for their children and gets great satisfaction in seeing them succeed; we happen to have eight unique, hard-working, good people, some of whom have gone on to reach great heights on the rugby field. They're all special and Robyn and I are immensely proud of each of them; what Beauden's been able to achieve is thanks in no small part to the love and support of his brothers and sisters.

As good a rugby player as he has become, it's the professionalism he displays on and off the field, the pressure he takes on his shoulders, the career he has chosen to have and the person he is every day that makes me most proud.

He's still our boy from the coast and that will never change.

Kevin Barrett

Introduction

I used to be called Rabbit.

When I was a kid, I had skinny legs, big ears and was good at cross-country. I can still hear my nana and aunty yelling 'Run, Rabbit!' or 'Go, Rabbit' as I'd charge off around the farm or at an athletics event. It wasn't a name I loved, but I can see why it stuck . . . and it does still come out from time to time.

I was always quite small, and to me All Blacks were like giants. The idea that I could ever be like those men seemed a crazy dream: nice to think about, fun to pretend to be Andrew Mehrtens or Christian Cullen in the backyard, but not at all realistic.

That sense of realism is probably the benefit of coming from a big family — having seven brothers and sisters can give a person perspective. When there are that many kids there's no chance anyone is going to let you get ahead of yourself and there's always someone to make sure you keep it real. Yes, we've always celebrated the wins and successes, but there are also going to be times that are tougher and a bit darker; keeping that perspective was always ingrained in us, was part of how we were brought up and the way we live our lives.

My love of the game comes from exactly the same place as it does for most kids. Playing on the farm with my brothers, Force Back on the school fields, coming up with moves when I should have been paying attention in class, and watching the All Blacks. It also very much comes from my dad who spent many years playing for Taranaki and the Hurricanes, and who taught me all the basics when I was young. Dad's advice and skill lessons were very influential, and I've adapted some of his techniques, tips and drills in the Skills section of this book.

It doesn't seem like there was much time between working on those basics with Dad and playing in the backyard with my brothers, to fulfilling

BARRETT FAMILY COLLECTION

'Run, Rabbit' was a familiar call when I was a kid.

that crazy dream and becoming an All Black. I finished high school at the end of 2009 and less than three years later made my test debut midway through 2012. In reflecting on this period in my career rather than what's happened since my first test, I've been reminded of what a whirlwind it was and that it felt just that.

For me, playing rugby was probably the easiest part. At every level of every sport we have all of those skills, drills and ways to practise and improve our game, but off the field, and in life generally, there isn't really a manual on how to do things. There sure wasn't for me when I was 19 and signing on to be a professional rugby player; it hasn't all been plain sailing and I've made plenty of missteps along the way. Despite that, I wouldn't change anything I've done, and I've learned to deal with the ups and downs in a positive way. All of those experiences have helped me get to where I am.

Like having a rugby coach, there are always people willing to help and guide you along the way and I hope I can give you some insights into some of the steps I've taken off the field, how I've had many people play a big part in supporting me and how I've been able to chase my dreams.

It's a long way from Pungarehu to having lunch with Richie McCaw on your first day as an All Black, but if a kid called Rabbit found a way to fulfil his dreams I hope you can find a way to achieve yours.

Beaudy

ROB TUCKER

CHAPTER 1
Family, farm & footy

Down the four kilometres of Lower Parihaka Road, at one of the westernmost points of New Zealand, lies a little slice of paradise. You can see Mount Taranaki on one side, the rugged coast on the other, and on occasion, Uncle Phillip's cows in the paddock outside the bedroom window. With cloudless days and beautiful pink sunsets that reflect off the mountain's snowy peak, there's a little bit of magic about it and it's where I feel most at peace.

It's the place I grew up and the place I call home.

While it is incredibly peaceful, it has always been a place where a lot of hard work gets done. It's busy and boisterous, but not noisy despite the comings and goings, and there's always something happening — just what you'd expect from a family of 10.

My parents Robyn and Kevin always intended to have plenty of kids, well Mum certainly did, and Dad was already from a big family anyway so it's possible he didn't get much of a say. So, here we are, in order of appearance: Kane, me, Scott, Blake, Jordie, Jenna, Zara and Ella. There's about 15 years between Kane the eldest and Ella the youngest and I was born in May 1991, 13 months after Kane and 16 months before Scott. My name comes from the French 'beau' which means 'handsome'. It's true; just ask my mum.

Our 'neighbourhood' in Pungarehu, about half an hour from New Plymouth, is seven dairy farms down the entire stretch of road that leads to the Tasman Sea and is a little community that included our cousins Josh and Neesha next door and the Crowleys, Daniel, Logan and Anna, up the road. Uncle Phillip (whose cows are sometimes stationed outside my bedroom window) has the farm closest to the beach and ours is the next one up. Dad is the third generation of his family to farm the land after his father and grandfather, buying the farm off Granddad Ted in 1993.

Parihaka itself holds a very important place in New Zealand's history as the centre of passive resistance against confiscation of Māori land in the 1860s and the site of an invasion in 1881. That part of the country

BARRETT FAMILY COLLECTION

Left: Me aged two. **Right:** Mount Taranaki forms the backdrop as the Barrett kids line up for a photo. **From left** — Ella, Zara, Jenna, Jordie, Blake, Scott, me and Kane.

has a very rugged, rocky coastline and is hard to farm with drought conditions and a lot of wind, but the coast itself turned out to be quite a good training ground. It's about 150 metres down to the low-tide mark so we used to run out to get pāua, jumping and stepping from boulder to boulder, which were quite slippery and a good test of our agility. Mum grew up about 15 minutes down the road in Opunake and her brother, my Uncle Ross, is still on the family farm there; we are a Taranaki family through and through.

Sport was at the centre of just about all we did and we were encouraged to give everything a go. I always had a ball in my hand, was organising the other kids or asking the school teacher if we could go out for a game of some sort, and our birthday and Christmas presents were usually sport related rather than any flash toys or gadgets. When we were small, Mum would set us off for races around the house, which were very competitive, always timed with a stopwatch and sometimes resulted in collisions when we went in opposite directions. If the sun was still up, there was no way we were sitting inside watching TV.

If we weren't playing rugby, there was athletics, cricket, basketball, swimming and golf as well as netball and Highland dancing for the girls. We keenly followed the Black Caps on TV and cricket was probably the number two sport for most of us, Jordie in particular, who played to a high level until quite recently. Despite growing up on one of the country's famed coasts with some of the best beaches around, Scott is the only one who ever really got into surfing, although we did go to Surf Club.

All three of the girls are talented netballers. Jenna plays in the grade below the professional domestic competition and it seems to be the sport that Ella, who's quite naturally gifted, is drifting most towards. Nothing stops Zara, who has Down syndrome, from being as competitive as the rest of us and she is a confident shooter in netball and a strong swimmer. She's also the most honest and stubborn of all of us — if any of us try to pick a fight with Zara, chances are we're going down. Dancing is definitely a talent and skill that only the girls in our family have; the rest of us are terrible and the only way we'd ever give it a go was for a laugh. All the timing and ability in that department went to Zara and Ella, and the rest of us don't have a drop of rhythm in our veins. It's in everyone's best interests if I stick to golf as a pastime and leave the dance floor to them.

Granddad Bob, Mum's dad, introduced us to golf even though he didn't start playing until he'd picked up a few books and decided to teach himself before passing it on to us. I was probably the keenest but Blake, who is a handy all-round athlete and tough as nails, is also a good golfer. Scott played a lot as well before he fell in love with the squat rack in his late teen years, started drinking lots of Dad's organic milk and became a massive unit! Granddad Bob is left-handed and when I picked up his clubs it felt quite natural so that's the way I learned. Despite the fact I'm right-handed I play golf left-handed as well as anything else that involves hitting a ball; in cricket I bat left-handed, but I bowl right-handed! Nana Barb was also a devoted teacher and participant in our games. The two of us would spend hours together, with her hitting a ball with a tennis racket and me catching it over and over, neither of us ever getting bored. We were lucky to be surrounded by proud and dedicated grandparents who nurtured our love of sport and had a big hand in keeping us grounded and connected as a family.

We were always taught, or rather told, to be good sports. When we took up golf, Mum threatened us that she would snap our clubs in half if we ever got stroppy or didn't follow the proper etiquette. Because Pungarehu primary was so small we had to make up our teams with lots of different ages and abilities so we learned that everyone was doing the best they could and the less sporty kids were helping us be able to field a team.

Three Barrett boys in the front row of this Pungarehu School photo — Kane (second from left), cousin Joshua (centre, captain) and me (far right). Dad (inset) was the coach. We were proud winners of the McLeod Shield.

BARRETT FAMILY COLLECTION

Even though we've always been competitive, sport was mostly about enjoyment. I loved competing and seeing improvement, and getting better at each element or faster at the 400 metres was a constant challenge. But as much as I loved all the sports I played, rugby was always my game. There's something about team sports that I've enjoyed; perhaps it's having that collective vision, working with your mates towards the same goal, sharing moments and being on the rollercoaster together. I have no doubt though that playing those different sports and learning a wide variety of skills helped me be a better rugby player.

If rugby was my game, Andrew Mehrtens was my guy, the one I'd try to copy in the backyard. He wasn't the biggest player, but he was very skilful and I loved his calm demeanour on the field, even though he might not have been the most physically talented guy out there. I loved Christian Cullen's gliding runs and explosive style as well; he also wasn't very big either, but I'm told he was extremely strong for his size and, like me, was from a small town. Cully was electric.

BARRETT FAMILY COLLECTION

Rugby was my game and Andrew Mehrtens was my guy. Kane and I got to meet Mehrts at Rugby Park, New Plymouth in 1998.

As well as mimicking Mehrts in the backyard, I also tried to copy his off-field style — if you could call it style. The only hairdo I had for years was a Mehrts bowl cut with a bit of an undercut for good measure, just like the one he rocked for a good couple of seasons. I'm sure the hairdresser was reluctant to give it to me and my hairstyles took a long time to improve; I reckon it's a bit of a Taranaki thing, a badge of honour, to have dirty knees, a terrible haircut and be throwing a rugby ball around. Besides, back then it was all about impressing the boys not the girls.

One of the most important aspects when we were young, if not the most important part of having a lot of siblings and close neighbours, is that we always had great numbers for backyard footy or whatever game we were going to play. Number six, Jenna, was a well-anticipated arrival into the family I'm sure, in the hope that after five boys we'd get a girl. But the main priority for Kane, Scott and me, of course, was that number six

BARRETT FAMILY COLLECTION

Left: Mud slides were all part of our kick-chase games on the farm. **Right:** A lineout skills session — Barrett boys style.

would mean an even number for the games; we could play three on three fairly once Jenna and the younger boys were big enough.

We'd work with whatever numbers we had and every day there'd be some form of competition. Two on two, or three on three, grubbers, kick-chase games where we'd create a massive mud slide down the lawn, kicking competitions and whatever else we could come up with. There was no way anyone was ever going to fully tackle Jenna whenever she got the ball because she was the cute little sister, but she was a great ball distributor and has excellent skills, even if we did have to convince her to play a bit more as she got older.

If Jenna was the good sport and indulged us at times by being that sixth player we needed, Jordie was not.

As the youngest of the boys he was always the pesky little brother wanting to hang out when I had friends over. I'd sometimes feel a bit bad because we'd bully him and he'd go off crying to Mum, and as I got older I felt more and more guilty, but he was just so annoying and I wanted to hang out with my mates. He was quite a cute little kid, but we knew how to push his buttons. We could see his blood starting to boil, he'd go as red as a beetroot and eventually he'd either start swinging or start crying!

Scott and I both had, and still have, pretty calm demeanours, while Kane was an aggressive rugby player but gentle off the field and Blake, like Jordie, had a bit of a fiery streak. We'd get into small scraps but never

BARRETT FAMILY COLLECTION

Kane (headgear) and me playing for the Okato under-12s, 2003.

full-blown punch-ups. There were lots of wrestles and more than a few swinging arms, but it would only be on very rare occasions that it would carry on inside and Dad would have to sort it out; we have always been such good mates as well as being brothers that we've never really fought. At least that's my side of the story; Blake and Jordie, the two youngest boys, might have a different version of events.

Up until I was about eight, both Mum, who was a good netballer and basketballer, and Dad were also still playing top-level sport, so if we weren't at school, working on the farm, or at our own games we were watching them play. The logistics of getting everyone where they needed to go are quite mind-boggling now that I think back on it. Kane and I spent a lot of time together as there's only 13 months' age difference between us and I'd always play up a year in his rugby teams, while Blake and Jordie are also only separated by around a year, so they played in the same teams together. It really helped the car-pooling. Scott in the middle thankfully had our good mates up the road and he'd jump in one of their cars, but often the grandparents and aunties did their fair share of shuttling us around as well. We had a supportive community where everyone mucked in and helped each other, especially when Mum and Dad couldn't spread themselves thin enough.

It was always busy and there was rarely a moment to pause, which made dinner around the table together every night pretty much a non-negotiable and was our time to catch up. Mealtimes and trips to church every Sunday morning were about the only time you'd get us all in one place. We had a big Ford station wagon, an eight-seater, which we'd pile in and out of as we headed up the road to church, which was fortunately not far away as the seatbelt wearing was a little loose in those days. However, contrary to what most people imagine, with a big family things were fairly structured with lots of routine when we were little — homework, dinner, shower and pyjamas — until one of us would suggest going out for 'one more' quick game of touch or cricket. That sometimes meant having to endure another round of knee scrubbing to avoid dirtying the clean bed sheets; the dirt levels on our shins and knees were always a good indication of how tough the game had been and there were times our knees were so raw and the dirt so ingrained, we'd be in tears as blood seeped through while we tried to scrub it off in the shower.

Keep in mind that during this time Dad was still playing top-level rugby in what were the early days of professionalism, including travelling to Wellington to be with the Hurricanes. Some days, if Taranaki were training at 4.30 in the afternoon, he'd have to be out the door before 4 pm, leaving Mum to finish off milking the cows, hose down the shed and get everything done for the day on the farm, as well as wrangling, at that stage, the six of us. We were all expected to pitch in to keep the cogs turning. That many mouths to feed meant a lot of potatoes to peel and I was Mum's sous chef, peeling, prepping and cleaning in the kitchen while the other boys were helping Dad outside or getting the cows in. They were a bit more suited to the 'dirty jobs' and I was quite good at being first in the door after school to see the list of chores, manipulate it to suit me and delegate the least-favourable tasks to the others.

Our parents, with the help of our grandparents, extended family and friends, just always made things work and got on with what needed doing. Mum's work ethic is to be admired and I think it's something she instilled in me. She's very hard-working to the point where she struggles to relax if she ever gets away for a rare holiday. She would be reasonably stern with us when we needed it and she's very determined but 100 per cent supportive and incredibly loving. Also, her scones are second to none.

§

Many years earlier, Mum and Dad had looked into overseas rugby contracts, but nothing came of it and when Dad eventually retired in 1999, he'd had enough of rugby. But they couldn't resist the opportunity

GETTY IMAGES

Dad celebrating Taranaki's win over Waikato at the 'Bull Ring' in New Plymouth towards the end of 1998. He played one more season for Taranaki before the family headed off to Ireland.

which arose shortly after to manage a dairy farm in Ireland with a bit of footy on the side. With six kids in tow, Jenna being just 18 months old, we headed off in January 2000, for a somewhat different kind of OE to what most people experience. We lived in a small parish called Ballinacree in County Meath, just over an hour's drive north of Dublin. The parish had a church, school, general store and a couple of bed factories while about five kilometres up the road was a bigger town, Oldcastle, which had a population of no more than 1000 people but was home to 13 pubs.

Our school at home, Pungarehu primary, had about 60 kids, three classrooms and one school bus, and the one we went to in Ireland, St Fiach's National School, was close to the same size but that's where the similarities ended. In Ireland, we had a traditional school uniform, which to my, Kane and Scott's horror included having to wear shoes and socks — a completely foreign concept for us! I found out the hard way on the first day that they were non-negotiable too when I thought nothing of whipping them off at morning interval to kick a soccer ball around, despite it being the middle of winter. Mrs McCormick, my new teacher, wasn't overly impressed to see a barefoot Kiwi kid and dismissed my protests that I really didn't need the shoes, much to my outrage. Even stranger for us than having to wear shoes in the first place was that you took them off before going into the classroom and popped on a pair of slippers!

Despite the rule about shoes it was a great school, very traditional and disciplined in its way of teaching and learning, and I'm sure when I got home later I was a lot smarter than my peers because of it. Every afternoon we had milk deliveries dropped off by a 'wee lorry' (what we'd call a small truck!), which I absolutely loved. We adapted to life in Ireland quite quickly.

Of course, we got stuck into playing sport over there as well. I really enjoyed Gaelic football, a fast and skilful game for which you need good endurance and where Dad's lessons about kicking off both feet proved vital. It was great for my hand-eye coordination and vision, being able to see space on the field. Dad had a crack as well, but let's just say he was probably a bit rough and physical and developed a reputation for introducing the 'fend' into it. I got really into soccer too, developing a love

BARRETT FAMILY COLLECTION

St Brigid's GAA Club Gaelic football team, 2000. That's me on the far right of the front row.

for Manchester United and Irishman Roy Keane, thinking I was going to become a professional footballer like him and make millions. I desperately wanted a pair of adidas Predator boots like David Beckham and once I got my hands on some, they would be my boots of choice for years to come. We played rugby for Mullingar and spent our weekends watching Dad turn out for the Buccaneers in Athlone and the All Ireland competition.

Our time in Ireland was an amazing life experience for a nine-year-old, getting a taste of a different community, culture and country, and I made lifelong friends.

Sixteen months in Ireland were followed by 16 months of another new experience once we got home. Mum and Dad had decided to rebuild the main farmhouse which meant we lived in the farm cottage while the build was happening. Mum, Dad, six of us, rather seven of us, as baby Zara arrived during this time, squeezing into the three-bedroom cottage made for quite a highlight. Mum reckons it was fine, just a place to put our heads since we didn't spend a lot of time inside anyway, and nothing that couldn't be fixed by a few sets of bunk beds and living a bit lightly for a while. But it was such a treat when we moved into the big new house where I had my own room for the first time and we had a massive rumpus room at our disposal as well. The fire still roars in winter and often there are scones in the oven.

It was around this time, returning from Ireland and in the final year at Pungarehu primary, which went up to year 8 (and incidentally was shut down by the Ministry of Education in 2003, much to my horror), that rugby started to take on a new level of importance for me. Because Dad was well known in the region, I'd always tried hard and taken rugby seriously in order to make him proud, but it was making the Taranaki under-13s for under-60 kilos where it became quite a big deal. I thought I was very cool in my black jacket with the Taranaki emblem on it and wore it everywhere. Making that team gave me a real boost as I was heading to boarding school at Francis Douglas Memorial College where there would be more competition for places and a bigger pool to select from.

I loved boarding school. I got to hang out with my mates 24/7 and we could get up to a bit of mischief — nothing really bad or naughty that would get us in serious trouble, but usually anything that would wind up the dorm supervisor. I was quite good at initiating the mischief and then managing to slip away at the right time, being smart enough or quick enough to leave my mates to get caught. It was always worth it even if we did have to do a lot of dishes as punishment. When it came to schoolwork and in the classroom, I would say I was 'good enough', certainly not a star student, but I got by even though I wasn't all that good at studying or focusing on what I should be. Quite often I'd be drawing rugby moves or coming up with plays on my notepad instead.

The great thing about boarding school was I didn't have the chores to do as I would at home so there was lots of spare time to play sport. After school, I would spend hours bowling in the cricket nets with my mates, playing Force Back or practising goal-kicking with my homemade tees.

BARRETT FAMILY COLLECTION

A proud member — middle row, third from right — of the Taranaki Primary Schools restricted weight team of 2004. We won the big quadrangular tournament that year and also beat Wellington for the first time.

I would cut a 600 ml Coke bottle in half, put it up through a cone, wrap it with insulation tape so it wouldn't move, then trim it up to get the angle and height I wanted. It was a more precise way than kicking the ball out of a shoe, and I spent plenty of time making them durable, getting the right colours and making them look good. I loved practising kicking and having competitions with my mates, seeing how far we could nail a goal from and trying to emulate Andrew Mehrtens. There's something therapeutic about going down to the park to kick balls and my homemade tees were things of beauty.

Rugby in my first two years at FDMC was played in weight divisions, but one big game was the focus in year 9 —the Boarders Cup. The year 13s would take us for training three times a week at 6.30 am to prepare us for the big match against New Plymouth Boys' High boarders. For two terms we underwent gruelling training sessions which included hill sprints, fitness work, and punishments if we weren't doing what we

BARRETT FAMILY COLLECTION

The Francis Douglas Memorial First XV of 2008. I'm kneeling on the far left of the middle row and Kane is fifth from left in the back row.

were supposed to; having to hold an electric fence was one and my mate Jarrod Crowley had to crawl through a drain as another! One of the year 13s, Shane Cleaver, who would go on to play for Taranaki and the Chiefs, was massive and scary. That's why we trained so hard because there was absolutely no way we were going to let down a guy like Shane and there was great prestige in impressing the big boys.

The game that year was being played at Boys' High and their ground known as The Gully. It's an intimidating scene when the entire school lines the grass terraces and does their haka, but we took real pride in standing up to the big schools. We won the Boarders Cup 8–5 in 2005.

That would be my only success at The Gully and against Boys' High. Blake, Jordie and Scott all managed to beat them when they were in the First XV, but it remains a black mark for Kane and me, who played two years together in the Firsts. The closest we came was when I was in year 11, my first season in the top team; it was a daunting prospect for a skinny fifth former to be taking on the big kids from up the road. We drew 25-all. A draw. I'd rather have lost trying.

Even as a young year 11 playing in a big game like that, I was able to keep control of my nerves fairly well. I generally feel about half nervous and half excited; sometimes there was a bit of anxiety, but I was always told to turn those nerves into a positive. It may also have been during my First XV days that I developed my one and only game-day habit. I'm not at all superstitious and don't have a list of rituals because I don't see the point in creating something else to worry about, but for some reason or other I have to put my right boot on first. It's just become a habit more than anything and never has nor ever will make any difference to how I play.

Francis Douglas Memorial College had about 750 boys from year 7 through to 13, so it was far from one of the big prominent rugby schools. In the years I played First XV we were very fit and skilful but often didn't have the playing numbers or the size of some of the other schools we matched up against; we would try to not be intimidated hearing the

BARRETT FAMILY COLLECTION

With Dad and former Francis Douglas student Conrad Smith after the 50th jubilee Old Boys match in 2009.

names and reputations of our opponents. Palmerston North Boys' High had an exciting fullback called Gillies Kaka and this guy who could play number eight or centre, Ngani Laumape. For us, it was quite humbling knowing we didn't have the resources of others, that we had to make do with what we had and come together as a tight team. We didn't always win against the likes of Palmy Boys', Feilding Ag or Napier Boys', and sometimes we got well and truly thumped, but when we did win it was very satisfying and we took great pride in standing up to schools that sometimes had twice the number of students we did.

From Pungarehu to Ireland, Francis Douglas, the farm cottage and then the big house, from having one awesome big brother to six great younger siblings, rugby, cricket, athletics and golf, Mum's scones and Dad's rugby lessons, my childhood and school years were fortunate and fun, and it was a very simple lifestyle. Like all families, we had our ups and downs, it wasn't perfect and there were difficult moments, but my upbringing was full of love and support, setting me up for the next phase of my life.

ROB TUCKER

CHAPTER 2
The Naki & 7s

I always wanted to play for Taranaki.

It's such a unique and special union, with a deep, rich history and some very proud clubs who contribute so much to the community. Going to see Dad play at Yarrow Stadium was always a great day out, not least because the mascot Ferdinand the Bull would throw loaves of bread into the crowd.

From a young age, rugby was clearly in our blood and something we were always involved in. We'd go to practice with Dad and spend time sitting on the roof of the clubrooms or up trees retrieving all the balls — and often going home with more balls than we'd started with. Like many kids, I'd dream of being an All Black, but it was hard to imagine it could truly happen. Playing for Taranaki, on the other hand, felt possible — I'd seen it in front of my own eyes, and watching Dad had given me something to aspire to.

But there was a time when it may not have happened.

As I was finishing up at Francis Douglas Memorial College, I was at a bit of a crossroads about what I wanted to do. At various stages through school, I had thought about becoming a physio for a sports team, studying law or going to Police College in Porirua; the only thing I knew for sure was that I was absolutely not going to be a dairy farmer — as much as I had loved growing up on the farm.

Going to university in Dunedin was shaping up as the best option as that's where a lot of my mates were heading, but there was a second possibility I considered: a move to Melbourne to play Aussie Rules.

Brother Peter Smyth was a teacher and rugby coach at FDMC and an all-round sports nut. He was originally from Australia, so Aussie Rules was his passion. He loved the idea of one of his students potentially playing in the AFL and had made a few enquiries about me going to a college in Melbourne, perhaps for a bit of study or to have a gap year and play footy. I was interested. During the school holidays, I went to a training camp with the Central AFL team in the Waikato and really enjoyed it; the passing and offloading skills were tricky but the kicking into space and running aspect of the game came quite naturally. I've always enjoyed the game and it's similar in nature to Gaelic football, which I played when the family lived in Ireland.

I had also missed out on the New Zealand Schools rugby team at around that time. While I was disappointed, I wasn't hugely surprised not to have made the cut. The first-fives selected were Lima Sopoaga ('Sops') and Gareth Anscombe who were at bigger schools, had more opportunity to stand out and deserved to be there as they were obviously being exposed to better rugby. It was always going to be difficult coming from a smaller school and having to play a key position in a trial situation when I didn't have any other teammates alongside me or natural combinations. I was always quite shy and nervous in that setting, whereas Sops was bubbly and exuberant, able to express himself and was confident to run a team.

I wouldn't say I was disillusioned with rugby after missing out on the Schools team, but having also had limited game time in the Hurricanes Schools team prior to that, I was perhaps a little disgruntled and somewhat in two minds about where my sporting direction lay. So there was enough interest there to give the Melbourne/Aussie Rules experiment decent thought. It would have been a really gutsy move to make and Brother Smyth was encouraging, but in reality, the idea of going to uni in Dunedin with my mates and living the student life was more enticing. I hadn't given up on rugby and perhaps going down south would give me a chance at it through their provincial and rep rugby systems.

I was a late developer and not very big, so I always felt if I could stay patient, chip away and grow physically my time would come. I was in the Taranaki pre-academy in that final year of school, which helps the transition to the academy proper; it was managed by former player Michael Collins, who'd go on to be CEO of Taranaki and then the Chiefs. Mike and Clark Laidlaw, who was the coach and now guides the New

GETTY IMAGES

Sir Gordon Tietjens . . . 'I was too scared to even look at him.'

Zealand Sevens, suggested I give sevens training a go, and FDMC coach Tim Stuck convinced me that was a good idea.

It was a no-brainer really. Sevens suited my style and it would give me the chance to get used to playing against men while having a lot of space and ability to avoid too much contact. I thought it could be a really good way to get my foot in the pro-rugby door and stay fit over summer.

And stay fit I did. Sevens is a gruelling game. My first tournament for Taranaki was at Mount Maunganui in early January and even though I'd been running every morning while on holiday over New Year in Whangamata, it was a rude awakening. I spewed on the first day.

But I loved the freedom and space of sevens and enjoyed playing for Clark, who is very real, enjoys a laugh and has a positive coaching style but also tells it like it is. I grew massively in confidence and because I'd started to do a lot more weight training in addition to the hard work of sevens practice, I was beginning to notice physical gains and it's when I first started to find my speed.

I still had few expectations, though, when we went to Queenstown for the national tournament in mid-January (2010). I was just excited to go down south for the first time, to play in such an awesome set-up and in front of the TV cameras as well, which I hadn't done before. I wanted to do well, knowing my parents and grandparents were watching at home and there were more than just people at the ground to impress.

Sir Gordon Tietjens was the national coach at the time, the revered 'Mr Sevens' who'd discovered the talents of Jonah Lomu and Christian Cullen. I was too scared to even look at him, let alone talk to him, as he stood on the sideline staring at players with his little notebook in hand. I felt like a school kid wanting to be on my best behaviour when the principal was around.

It therefore came as a complete and utter shock when he named me in the national sevens squad. I was stoked to have simply been in the Taranaki team, so to hear Titch read my name out at the end-of-tournament dinner was beyond my wildest imaginings.

Selection in the New Zealand squad ended any idea of going to Melbourne and trying AFL; it also meant I had to weigh up whether going to uni in Dunedin was the right thing. I'd been given a massive opportunity to play sevens for New Zealand, so to really live the student life 'properly' would have been difficult, let alone trying to maintain the fitness levels Titch required. It may have been a tougher choice had I known exactly what I'd wanted to do at university, but I knew for sure that I was pretty passionate about rugby and a great chance was sitting there right in front of me. So instead of going down south with my mates (and, who knows, maybe eventually playing for Otago), I chose to stay at home on the farm and got an admin job with Origin Energy in New Plymouth. That also meant the dream of eventually playing for Taranaki was still on the cards.

Nowadays, the national sevens squad all live and train together at Mount Maunganui, but back then we would have camps throughout the season from which the squads for each tournament would be picked. Those camps were some of the most brutal sessions I've ever done. It was the well-known Titch way that everyone has heard about, but actually doing them was a total eye-opener . . . just when you thought it was over, he'd be yelling at you to go again. I thought I was fit, but no matter how fit you are, Titch knows how to break you.

The national sevens was quite a daunting step up for me, but Taranaki players Kurt Baker and Ben Souness were also in the squad and they took me under their wing. Kurt's a real character, so as things progressed and got more serious, he was a good person to still be able to have a laugh with off the field. It was certainly the support I needed when as a very raw, very green 18-year-old I was selected for the final two tournaments of the season in London and Edinburgh. As helpful as those guys were,

OPPOSITE: In action during my unexpected New Zealand Sevens debut, against Wales at the London tournament in 2010.

GETTY IMAGES

BARRETT FAMILY COLLECTION

With the Plate final trophy after the London Sevens, 2010.

they also stitched me up big time when I had my birthday on tour and they made me sing 'Happy Birthday' to myself in front of the team and other hotel guests. I barely said anything on the field, let alone saying boo off it, because I was so shy — and there I was singing to DJ Forbes, Tomasi Cama and Tim Mikkelson. Brutal.

I didn't get a heap of game time and the team struggled that season, but I still remember the feeling of racing 40 metres with my first touch to go in under the posts at Twickenham; the music was pumping, the crowd was full of London-based Kiwis and I'd scored. If this was what big-time rugby at one of the best stadiums in the world felt like, I was one hundred per cent into it.

That was when I realised making a career out of rugby was a realistic prospect. I missed out on selection for the squad which went on to win the gold medal at the Delhi Commonwealth Games later that year (some guy named Ben Smith decided to come back and play sevens), but given the aspirations I had to play for Taranaki I was ready to get stuck into fifteens. I'd gone from strength to strength and made the most of the few opportunities I'd had with the sevens team; I knew that if I really knuckled down now, this rugby business could become a permanent thing.

§

Colin Cooper was the new Taranaki coach in 2010 and had signed me up earlier in the year. He'd originally coached Taranaki from 1999, which was Dad's last year, and he had gone on to have success at the Hurricanes, including guiding them to the final against the Crusaders in 2006 — the infamous foggy final. I have lot of respect for Colin, but even so I had to weigh up whether I was ready to step up from schoolboy rugby to taking on some of the gnarly veterans of the national provincial competition. Although I'd been playing against men in sevens, I was still a bit daunted by the prospect of doing so in fifteens and moving into what I viewed as the big time. I say now I thought hard about it, but in reality it was only about a day of mulling it over before going back to Colin and being raring to get into training with Taranaki and potentially fulfilling the long-held ambition of playing for the Amber and Blacks.

I'd managed to get a couple of games in for the Coastal clubs under-20s and the Senior A team leading into the Taranaki campaign and it was so enjoyable. I love the culture of club rugby, how relaxed it can be but then how intense it gets as soon as it's time to play; everyone involved simply loves the game and is proud to play and represent the coast. It remains the only time I've been able to play for Coastal and even then it was a juggle with sevens training.

Those few games for Coastal didn't really prepare me, however, for how it would feel being part of the Taranaki team. Being in the NPC squad hit home once the Super Rugby players started to filter back into the squad; suddenly the likes of Jason Eaton and Craig Clarke were my team-mates, wearing the same kit as me as we trotted out for training. In less than 10 months I'd gone from finishing school and being uncertain about where I was heading, to the national sevens and world series circuit, to now having my name on a sticker in the changing room at Yarrow Stadium (which, incidentally, is still there).

Yarrow Stadium is electric when it's full. People pack in and have their favourite spots from where they watch each week; you can see Mount Taranaki from the northern terraces and it's just a great place to play footy. The province always comes out and supports the team and my debut in the opening game of the 2010 season against Northland was no different; it was close to a full house that day.

I was on the bench but thrown into it quite early due to an injury, and it was such a thrill hearing the cheer from my entire family and my friends in the crowd as I ran on to slot in at second-five — a position I'd never played in my life.

. . . And I was marking Rene Ranger.

A very special match programme — my debut game for Taranaki, against Northland at Yarrow Stadium, 2010.

JOHN VELVIN/ESPNZ

It was the first and last time I played second-five. Rene was at the peak of his powers and I was terrified. Before I knew it, the ball was out of their scrum and he was coming towards me; I thought he was going to try to beat me on the inside, but instead he did his little goosestep and fend and broke the line.

It felt then like it could be a long night, but the game flew by. We clawed back their big early lead, but Northland was too good and, just like that, my first game was over. There was no stopping, no time to look into the crowd or absorb the moment because I was so zoned in and everything felt electric; my senses were completely heightened. I could have played another three games that night.

A few weeks later, my brother Kane played his first game for Taranaki, coming off the bench against Otago on a cold and windy day at Carisbrook. It was a special game as I started at fullback for the first time in what would be the only time I'd play at the famous old ground. It was a very proud moment for all of us. To have two sons emulate their father by playing for a union we were so passionate about and had been so loyal to as a family still has great significance for us.

Growing up, we were aware of Dad's legendary status in the province and as we were reaching greater heights with our own rugby, his reputation as a hard-nosed Taranaki man became more apparent. That was something Kane and then Scott were far more equipped to live up to than I ever was. Kane was a very, very tough loose forward, whereas I was the first-five/fullback who was faster and more agile but hated tackling.

I think you either have that mongrel element to your game or you don't. You can work on it if you channel it, but I knew I didn't have that side to me and that's fine; I just had to find ways to get into a zone and make a mental switch to be as physical as possible or I'd get smashed.

OPPOSITE: Rene Ranger made the most of my inexperience at second-five, breaking through this attempted tackle in Taranaki's match with Northland in 2010.

For Dad and Kane, it was always there and they were quite fearless, while I was more hesitant going into contact because of my smaller stature. Kane was dominant and physical, much more in Dad's mould . . . although he'd never be able to get away with things on the field the way they did in Dad's day!

We both regularly came off the bench for the remainder of that first season and Kane can apparently lay claim to quite a record: possibly scoring the quickest try ever by a substitute when he crossed the line 16 seconds after coming on against Hawke's Bay.

I did get one more start. Going into the last game of the season, we still had an outside chance of making the semis if we could beat North Harbour and other results went our way. I was given the opportunity to start at first-five for the first time and in an afternoon game; it was an exciting chance to play some great running rugby with a dry ball.

They were the sort of conditions that produced a heck of a game. We won it 49–47 and I kicked 19 points, but that was far from the abiding memory as very early on Harbour pulled a set move that had me reeling. Their number eight Mat Luamanu peeled off the back of a lineout and had me lined up in his sights. He was huge; about 1.93 metres tall and 120 kilos whereas I was about 83 kg wringing wet . . . I stood my ground, tried to go high in the tackle and quite literally did a backflip as he pushed me off. Luamanu went on to score a hat-trick in the match.

I may have taken some knocks, but I loved my 10 to 20-minute cameos off the bench during that campaign, largely coming on at first-five to replace Willie Ripia late in a game. It would have been such a big ask to go straight from school into starting for an NPC team, so instead I was exposed to all the strategy groups and attack meetings to try to take in as much as possible during the week. Then I'd be let loose and given a

OPPOSITE: Looking to pass against North Harbour in a do-or-die match at Albany in 2010. It was my first start at first-five for the Naki and I managed 19 points as we sneaked home 49–47.

GETTY IMAGES

Trying to break the line against North Harbour, 2010.

chance to play with freedom for a short spell on the weekend. If Willie had been injured early in a game then, sure, I would have dealt with playing 70-odd minutes, but it was much easier to integrate off the bench and not spend too long overthinking things or have to make big decisions for an entire game.

Colin Cooper and Leo Crowley were fabulous coaches and had a big influence on me in that first season with Taranaki.

I spent a lot of time with Leo, watching footage and understanding his view of the game. He's quite a traditional coach but also very innovative

GETTY IMAGES

Leo Crowley and Colin Cooper were fabulous coaches who had a big influence on me in 2010.

and he has a real willingness to take on other people's feedback. Some coaches don't always buy into the ideas offered up by senior players, but Leo was an excellent facilitator who would also challenge those ideas and had a great outlook on how we played.

In a way, I felt the same about playing under Colin as I did about my father. Dad was never verbally hard on us, but we knew he had standards and we subconsciously wanted to live up to them. Despite his big smile and being quite softly spoken, I absolutely knew Coops was a very hard-nosed player so didn't want to let him down or have him thinking I was a bit soft. He helped me find my voice and confidence to be able to boss around the likes of Jason Eaton, Craig Clarke and Scott Waldrom, and to keep Kurt Baker in line.

Colin saw more in me than what I believed in myself at the time.

ROB TUCKER

CHAPTER 3

A whirlwind year

Midway through that first season with Taranaki in 2010, the interest started to come in from Super Rugby sides.

Even though I'd also been offered a sevens contract extension, I was aware from a tactical point of view that if I wanted to be playing first-five at a high level, I couldn't chop and change between sevens and fifteens. As soon as I'd started with Taranaki, it became clear that I was committed to fifteens and that's where I wanted to put my emphasis. There were two Super Rugby options, with two vastly different offers on the table.

The Hurricanes had been in contact fairly early and, having played for their Schools team and being from the region, I had been in their system, albeit loosely, for a while. Assistant coach Alama Ieremia and high-performance manager Jono Phillips wanted to put me on a wider training group contract and treat 2011 as a development year. On the other hand,

GETTY IMAGES

Making a break against Auckland in the final of the 2011 National Sevens tournament in Queenstown. Despite being offered a sevens contract extension, fifteens was always going to be the choice for me.

the Blues were offering a fast track to the big time: a full contract with serious opportunities to play regularly at the top level and about three times the money of the Hurricanes deal. We went up to Auckland to meet with the Blues and toured Eden Park. It was very tempting.

The view of many is that the step up from NPC level to Super Rugby is greater than the jump from Super to the international game. Colin Cooper had been very mindful of my development with Taranaki. He could have thrown me in the deep end and I would have been gone as quickly as I arrived, but his approach probably helped guide my thinking when it came to choosing the best option for the next steps. I was working hard in the gym, learning a lot about the game, and he could see I'd be running a team in the next year or so, but Coops also knew the demands of Super Rugby.

Even though I had progressed quickly, I just knew deep down I wasn't ready to be spearheading a Super Rugby team straight away. Some

BARRETT FAMILY COLLECTION

With Dad after a match for the Hurricanes Schools side in 2009. I chose to stick with the Canes when it came to Super Rugby.

19-year-olds are fully grown, big and developed, but it's rare to see them playing in a position of such responsibility as I was. I needed more time.

Although there was a massive difference money-wise between the two offers, it was almost irrelevant. I knew if I knuckled down and worked on my development, it would pay off in the long run and the financial rewards would come eventually. So, I signed with the Hurricanes for about $45,000 and thought I was minted.

Helping with the negotiations and weighing up the best option was my manager at the time Ashley Smith. Dad was very involved too as he'd been through it right at the start of professionalism in the mid-1990s, and Mum would pop in and out just enough to keep aware of the conversations, but Ashley really drove that process. He'd been helping our family out for a while and was very thorough, challenging the franchises as to how they were going to deliver the development I needed. Too often we see players get exposed at a young age and thrown into it too early, particularly in positions like mine where you are charged with effectively driving the team and the game.

To make sure that didn't happen to me, we asked to have a set of clear expectations written up so I could see what the next two to three years could look like. These key performance indicators (KPIs) weren't put into the contract as such, but because it was all about development and I was taking a financial hit, they were documented so we all had a reference point. During the negotiations, the Canes were able to show where they thought they could take me in relation to those goals around the physical, mental, tactical, nutritional and technical sides of the game.

Ashley's approach was totally different to the traditional way of doing things back then and I'm sure very new and unique for the franchises to deal with. The Hurricanes may have been wondering who the heck this guy was at the start, but I think they saw how serious we were and how much we cared, as well as the reward in being accountable to each other. I'm really thankful to Ash for the process we went through.

Alama Ieremia, who was influential in helping to develop my attacking game.

Another big factor in opting for the Hurricanes was the obvious desire to follow in Dad's footsteps and create that legacy. Alama had played with and against Dad so we already had a connection, but he also sold the Hurricanes story pretty loudly! It helped also that he and I spoke the common language of golf, and Alama would become influential in helping develop my attacking game with his creativity and attention to detail.

I was the third cab off the rank when it came to the first-fives, behind Aaron Cruden, who'd made his All Blacks debut the year before, and Daniel Kirkpatrick who'd moved back to Wellington after a season with the Blues. Knowing where I stood helped me to focus immediately on where I needed to improve, without the pressure of being expected to play in game one. There was a lot of work to be done off the field and it was an eye-opener to be moving out of my comfort zone to the big city where there's a whole new world of support with nutritionists, professional development managers and trainers, as well as all the coaches.

David Gray was (and still is) the Hurricanes' head of physical performance, and he couldn't wait to get me into shape. A former Scotland Sevens international, Davie was very firm and expected nothing but excellence, although at the same time the scientific nature of being a trainer meant he was always learning something new and finding ways to get the best out of us. As a scrawny Naki boy who hated the gym, I was probably a bit of a project for him and the nutritionists who had a plan to get some weight on me. Super Rugby pre-season is incredibly hard work, and Davie was a very tough trainer . . . with all the food I was shovelling in as well, it didn't take long to see results.

I was also involved in the strategy and review meetings, taking in masses of information all the time, putting it into practise on the training field and getting feedback from Alama. I'd talk through game situations with Aaron Cruden, peppering him with questions about what he'd do in certain instances, why he had done something or what he was thinking at the time; things only other number 10s can answer. Although it can be daunting asking so much of an older player, we were encouraged to learn from each other, and while it really helped my development I hope it helped get the best out of Crudes as well . . . even if he did leave for the Chiefs the following season!

Being the third-string first-five meant I was training with the team every day, but when they'd have away games, I'd turn out for the development side. Often playing at what is now known as Jerry Collins

OPPOSITE: Aaron Cruden, who I peppered with questions back in 2011.

GETTY IMAGES

Stadium in Porirua where the southerly howls straight down the ground, it was good hard rugby and the best level I'd ever played at.

It all contributed to a massive shift physically and mentally in the eight months or so since the contracts were first being considered. It's hard training with the team and then having to watch them play week in, week out, sitting on the couch imagining what I'd be like if I was in Aaron's position and what I'd do differently. I'd gone from not believing I was ready to play Super Rugby, to knowing I absolutely was and that I wanted nothing else.

It took until round nine for the chance to come. Aaron was injured against the Brumbies and I was called into the squad to travel to South Africa for games against the Cheetahs and Sharks. I was excited, I was nervous, but I couldn't wait to get there.

My debut in Bloemfontein was 16 minutes off the bench in a typically frenetic, madcap game. We had a late comeback, with Jeremy Thrush scoring in the last play of the game to win it 50–47, and I kicked the conversion on the hooter for my first Super Rugby points. It was such a buzz, totally exhilarating.

The following week in Durban was more of a reality check as to what it's really like to play in South Africa. Talk about a step up. Playing the Sharks at Kings Park is so physical and so demanding; the ground is imposing, and we were completely up against it. I didn't get much game time, but I remember feeling we were outgunned, only scoring two tries in a 40–24 defeat.

I made two more appearances off the bench, playing at home the week after returning from South Africa in a last-gasp win over the Reds where Crudes kicked the winning penalty, and then again a few weeks later on a miserable night in Invercargill in what was an equally miserable loss to the Highlanders. It was a middling season overall for the Hurricanes,

OPPOSITE: I'm quick to congratulate Jeremy Thrush after he scored the match-winning try for the Hurricanes against the Cheetahs in my Super Rugby debut at Bloemfontein in 2011.

GETTY IMAGES

finishing ninth in a year best remembered for the feats of the Crusaders who played every game away from home following the Christchurch earthquake, only to fall just short in the final against the Reds.

Bubbling away while the Super Rugby campaign was ongoing was preparation for the under-20 World Cup. When I wasn't part of the Hurricanes, I'd be away at trials or camps for the 20s ahead of the tournament to be played in Italy in June, towards the end of Super Rugby.

Looking back now at the names in that team is quite something. Captained by Luke Whitelock, it featured among others Sam Cane, Brodie Retallick, TJ Perenara, Codie Taylor, Brad Weber, Lima Sopoaga, Waisake Naholo and Charles Piutau. Sixteen of the squad would go on to play international rugby, including Brad Shields for England, Gareth Anscombe for Wales and Ben Tamiefuna for Tonga. Mark Anscombe was the head coach with Chris Boyd, who would later coach me at the Canes, as his assistant and in charge of the backs.

I was expecting my first meeting with Chris to be quite serious, but he straight away said, 'How do you want to play? What do you want to do?' and gave me licence to be creative. It's an attitude I'd learn more about and admire about his coaching style — Chris just loves to see his teams play footy, not die wondering, and for players to express themselves. Yes, you still have to weigh up the risk against the reward of throwing the ball around and he'd always be able to show why an option was the right or wrong one, but the feeling we got was all about attacking and having fun with it. With the backline we had, it was all we needed to hear and because I'd had some Super Rugby experience, I was seen as one of the backline leaders.

New Zealand has an incredible history at the under-20 World Cup, which first began in 2008 after World Rugby merged the under-19 and under-21 age-grade systems. We'd won the tournament in each of the previous three years and we were well aware of that success and the expectations that came with it.

It feels like that history and Chris's 'licence to thrill' gave us the

GETTY IMAGES

Attacking for New Zealand Under 20 in our opening pool match against Wales at Rovigo, Italy, 2011.

Making a break against Argentina in our third pool match at the World Rugby Under 20 Championship in 2011.

GETTY IMAGES

confidence to play the rugby we did in that tournament and we had a total blast, scoring 204 points in pool play and conceding just 22 before going on to beat Australia fairly comfortably in the semi-final. Such was the depth of our team, many of us had been playing out of position and that was no different in the final. With Gareth at first-five, Lima played at 12 with Francis Saili outside him, meaning Charles Piutau was on the wing and I was at fullback — it's a measure of the team that Waisake couldn't get a start and came off the bench in the final.

It's fair to say the England side we played in the decider was somewhat handy as well. Featuring Owen Farrell, Elliot Daly, Mako Vunipola and George Ford, they were quite hardened after coming through a difficult pool phase and a tricky semi-final against France, and, of course, any England team is desperate to end New Zealand dominance. They were gunning for us.

England flew out of the blocks with an early try before we were able

Scoring one of New Zealand's three tries in our win against England in the final of the World Rugby Under 20 Championship in Padova.

to get ourselves into the game. While we took control, it got really tight midway through the second half when they came back within one point and missed the conversion that would have put them in front. Looking back, we probably just had too much firepower and Gareth kicked superbly that day, while I scored the try to finish it off; if it was half the match to watch as it was to play in, the 10,000 or so in the stands in Padua were given a great final. We were elated, winning a World Cup and continuing four years of dominance for New Zealand while playing a brand of rugby that we loved.

A celebratory haka after our World Rugby Under 20 Championship win over England in 2011.

GETTY IMAGES

GETTY IMAGES

Winners are grinners . . . posing with the trophy and our medals — after the World Rugby Under 20 Championship final.

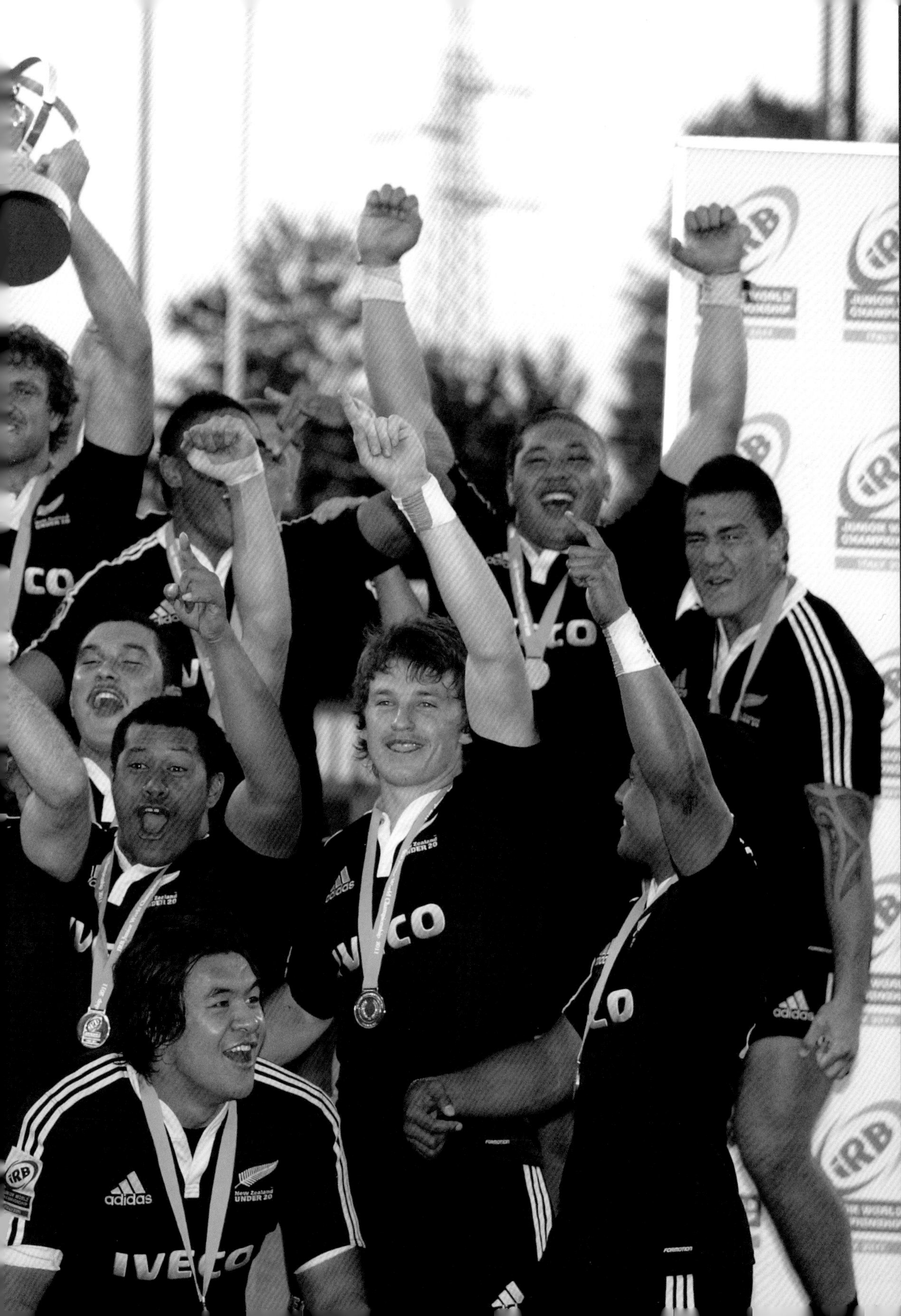
adidas
New Zealand
UNDER 20
IVECO

§

On 24 August 1996, Dad helped Taranaki win the Ranfurly Shield. Fifteen years to the day, on 24 August 2011, I did the same.

The oldest trophy in New Zealand provincial rugby, the history and tradition of the Ranfurly Shield means it is still coveted by players and unions today. There are legendary stories of the challenges, defences and celebrations, and every rugby fan knows the part their team has played in maintaining the heritage of the Shield.

Nineteen ninety-six was the first year of professional rugby in New Zealand, the Blues had won the inaugural Super Rugby competition and Auckland had been the dominant provincial team for years. They'd held the Shield for a record 61 successful defences through until 1993 and regained it towards the end of the '95 season. It was very much seen as the big-money union from the big smoke against the rural dairy farmers when Dad's team went up to challenge for the Ranfurly Shield.

It was a pulsating game, back and forth between the teams in front of a good crowd at Eden Park, including many travelling Naki fans. Taranaki won the match 42–39 and Dad actually had the final touch of the ball, spilling it over the tryline, thumping his fists on the ground and then, seconds later, raising them in the air when he heard the final whistle.

Few in New Plymouth will forget the image of the gap-toothed Taranaki icon Andy Slater stepping off the plane and raising the Shield aloft. I was five at the time and we'd stayed home to watch on TV, so we headed to the airport with hundreds of others to meet Dad and the team off the plane, and later we had the Shield out at the farm. They had one successful defence a week later before losing it to Waikato, and by the end of that '96 season the Shield had found its way back to Auckland.

The circumstances in 2011 were much different. Our challenge was against Southland in Invercargill, kicking off at 8 pm on a Wednesday, and it came just four days after we'd been thrashed 27-nil by

BARRETT FAMILY COLLECTION

A proud Barrett family pose with Dad and the Ranfurly Shield after Taranaki's historic win over Auckland in 1996.

Canterbury! As you'd imagine, it was tight and tense with the scores going up in threes as my Southland opposite James Wilson and I traded penalties throughout. In the end, he kicked four out of five and I kicked five out of seven — that was it; the difference was one extra penalty as we won it 15–12. It didn't matter in the end, though, how we did it, all that counted was that the Shield was going back to the Naki for the first time since Dad's team had won it.

Unlike the '96 side, we had no time for parades and celebrations because our first defence was just four days later. If we could beat Hawke's Bay we'd hold on to the Shield for the summer and get to do the rounds and share it with everyone, but if we lost, it would be a new record for the shortest-ever Shield tenure. There was plenty at stake and the province knew it. Supporters packed into Yarrow Stadium that Sunday afternoon and seemed as determined as we were to do their bit to hold on to it. Hawke's Bay had a strong team that featured Brodie Retallick and my Hurricanes teammates Richard Buckman and Dan Kirkpatrick, but we were

GETTY IMAGES

BARRETT FAMILY COLLECTION

Just as Dad had done back in 1996, I was able to take the Ranfurly Shield back to the farm in 2011.

up for it and played really well to lock the Shield away for the summer.

The Ranfurly Shield is a huge part of our family's rugby history. Kane would have a big role in defending it throughout the 2012 season, and Scott and Jordie would go on to win it with Canterbury a few years later. Dad had started it all in 1996 and when we held on to it against Hawke's Bay, I got the chance to do what he had done and take the Shield back to the farm to celebrate.

It was the perfect way to finish a whirlwind year. I'd effectively had my first season as a full-time professional rugby player, won the under-20 World Cup and twice followed in Dad's footsteps by making my Hurricanes debut and winning the Shield.

Only a few years earlier, my aspirations had extended only as far as playing for the beloved Taranaki. Little did I know just how soon the biggest step up of all would come

OPPOSITE: Kicking one of five penalty goals in Taranaki's 15-12 Ranfurly Shield win over Southland in 2011.

Beauden Barrett's 'most played'

Dancing may not be my strong suit, but music has helped me through tough gym sessions and long bus rides, and to tune out and get focused for training or games. It's a mixed bag of generations and genres, but these songs are on high rotation.

Underwater
RÜFÜS DU SOL

Jungle
Tash Sultana

Skyline
(Alex Schulz Remix)
Möwe

Blinding Lights
The Weeknd

Treat you Better
RÜFÜS DU SOL

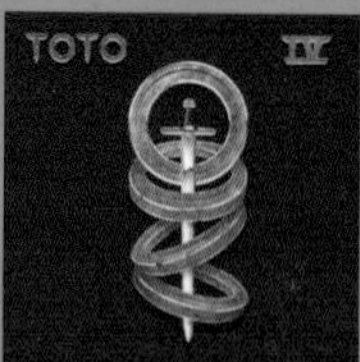

Africa
Toto

One (Live)
Shapeshifter

Born to Run
Bruce Springsteen

Born to Be Yours
Kygo & Imagine Dragons

Firestone
Kygo ft. Conrad

Hysteria
Def Leppard

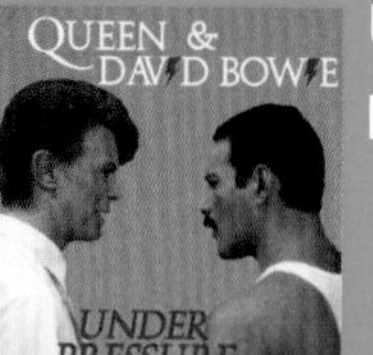

Under Pressure
David Bowie & Queen

Everywhere

Fleetwood Mac

I'm on Fire

Bruce Springsteen

In the Air

L.A.B.

Chameleon

PNAU

Forever

Six60

More than a Feeling

Boston

Monarch

Shapeshifter

Solid Gold

PNAU (Friction remix)

Rain

Dragon

You're the Voice

John Farnham

Stay

Kygo ft. Maty Noyes

Give & Take

Netsky

Right Here, Right Now

Fatboy Slim (CamelPhat remix)

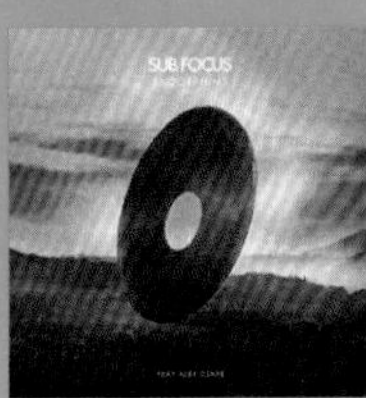

Endorphins

Sub Focus

Mr Brightside

The Killers

Jokerman

Bob Dylan

GETTY IMAGES

CHAPTER 4
All Black no. 1115

Hurricanes manager Tony Ward handed me the phone. We'd just come off the field against the Waratahs in Sydney and as he passed it over, he said, 'It's Darren Shand.'

My eyes widened. Darren Shand, the All Blacks manager. He was calling to tell me I'd been selected in the squad for the June series against Ireland.

Somewhere in between him telling me the news and that we would be assembling in Auckland the next day I might have said thanks and a few other words, but I was in such a state of shock not much more came out of my mouth. The skinny kid, once called Rabbit, from a farm in Pungarehu was going to be an All Black.

There was a great buzz going into the 2012 season. The All Blacks had won the World Cup months earlier, with the country hosting an awesome tournament, and everyone was on a high. For my part, I knew I had a great opportunity at the Hurricanes as Aaron Cruden had moved to the Chiefs, leaving me and Dan Kirkpatrick to vie for the starting 10 jersey. I was 10 kilos heavier than a year earlier, had gained a huge amount of tactical knowledge and was much more confident about running a game. We also had a strong and settled backline, anchored by two of the best communicators I've ever played with, Tim Bateman and Conrad Smith. Starting all but one game that season with those two outside me and one of the great talkers, Cory Jane, on the wing helped grow my game a lot; they gave information and direction — everything I needed at first-five.

It's not hard to do the maths that with five Super Rugby franchises and the likelihood they'd pick three first-fives in the All Blacks squad, I'd at least be able to get the selectors' attention given I was playing week in, week out for the Canes. Back then I also used to read and listen to a lot of the media chatter, absorbing everything about the game and what people were saying about me and my teammates. Nowadays I don't do that at all, as there's a lot more bad that comes with the good, but in 2012 when no one really gave me a chance, the tone was more positive; I found

With Conrad Smith — one of the best communicators in the business — at the start of the 2012 Super Rugby season.

it motivating. I wanted to prove people right, that, yes, I was good enough and ready for the next level.

Knowing I was likely to be in the frame didn't make the phone call from Darren Shand any less of a shock and going back into the changing sheds in Sydney after a good win over the Waratahs was surreal. Julian Savea, who'd also been picked for the first time, and I were obviously elated, but there were others in our team who were disappointed to have missed out, so there were a few mixed emotions. I got very little sleep that night and we were on an early flight the next morning to assemble on the North Shore.

We'd been asked to keep the news quiet until the squad was officially announced to the public and media the next day, but I did call Dad. He

GETTY IMAGES

doesn't usually say much on the phone anyway, and this time he really was speechless, but after a bit of a pause I could hear the pride and buzz in his voice. I was equally as proud to be able to tell him and Mum the news; they're the ones who really see the blood, sweat and tears, and while in the back of their minds they may have hoped for this, they still never really expected it.

I'll never forget my first day in the All Blacks camp as long as I live. Arriving at the team hotel from Sydney, Darren Shand ('Shandy') told me to grab some lunch and we'd meet later. When I walked into the restaurant there was only one other person there . . . Richie McCaw, eating lunch all alone. It would have been rude and a bit gutless not to join him, but I was incredibly nervous and there weren't too many words exchanged during that lunch.

Having made it through my first impromptu meeting with the All Blacks captain I then went upstairs and discovered I was rooming with Daniel Carter. While it was a little less intimidating than walking into lunch with Richie, I was still in awe when I saw bags with the initials 'DC' sitting there. The layout of the room was like an apartment where we each had our own rooms within it, so I went and hid out in mine for a bit to gather myself, leaving him to it after a brief initial conversation. It was a heck of an opening hour as an All Black.

Thankfully, there's plenty of admin for the first-timers as well, which probably saved me from any more awkwardness with my new roommate. There are a lot of people to meet, technical gear and software to get set up for the game plans, and going through all the personal info with Bianca Thiel, the executive assistant. And then there's the outfitting. I'm pretty sure every new All Black has described this as being like Christmas and there really is no other comparison.

OPPOSITE: Training at Beetham Park, Hamilton, just a few days out from my All Blacks debut in 2012.

Anyone would dream of being sponsored by adidas and getting all the kit and I was no different, laying it all out on my bed and taking photos; it was a far cry from Kane's hand-me-downs.

§

There's always a massive amount of scrutiny focused on any All Blacks team, but after the World Cup success and with Steve Hansen's appointment as head coach there were a lot of eyes on the first squad of 2012. It was evident that it was Steve's time and he certainly wanted to do things his way, which was reflected in the squad selected. It had an interesting dynamic and a great balance, with about eight key leaders returning and many others from the World Cup squad mixed with the newcomers; along with me and Julian Savea, Aaron Smith, Brodie Retallick, Sam Cane, Luke Romano and Ben Tameifuna had all been selected for the first time.

Steve set to work straight away to get everyone on the same page. There was no waiting for a campaign or two to settle in and enjoy the post-World Cup glow for those who'd been there. He connected with the team instantly and had everyone striving for the same mission about how to kick on from the World Cup and take things to the next level. Goals were set very early on that we wanted to be the most dominant team in history; in order to do that we needed to dominate the decade, and for that to happen we needed to work backwards from there. Ultimately, it will be up to others to decide if we became that team, but from the first days of Steve's first series against Ireland it was clear we could control how we wanted to perform. He had the key leaders on board and the rest of us followed their example and tried to live up to their standards.

That doesn't mean I wasn't absolutely terrified of Steve when I walked into that first camp! I was quite intimidated and initially struggled to have conversations with him, perhaps being aware he was a former police

Do I look nervous? It's my first All Blacks press conference, at Hamilton in 2012, alongside Steve Hansen and Luke Romano.

officer and feeling like I was the one in trouble. But as I got to know him and learned more about him, I found he was a big softy deep down and that he trusts his players to deliver. Like previous coaches, he possibly saw me as a bit of a project as well and knew it would take some prodding and testing me at training to see if I had the goods. With DC and Crudes both having had injury problems the previous seasons, Steve could have gone with a more experienced first-five as cover, but I guess he chose me with a view to the future, knowing it could take a bit of time. Steve values loyalty and as a player you wanted to prove him right. I'm grateful he stuck with me.

Along with Steve's vision of where he wanted to take the team, we newcomers saw how recent history and successes can motivate the current squad. Mental skills coach Gilbert Enoka does a brilliant job creating a team room in whatever hotel the squad is in around the world that reminds us of home and where we are from. It helps bring us back down to earth, connect each player with the vision, enhance the legacy and inspire us to continue it. The team room is our whare. Gilbert plasters the room with posters of recent players along with the campaigns they've been involved in. It's almost like an honours board where, for example, an image of Richie McCaw would have alongside it all the years he won the Bledisloe Cup, Rugby Championship, domestic series, grand slams or World Cups. The list of successes goes from city to city, country to country, and is awe-inspiring for any new All Black.

Going into the series with Ireland, Steve had said he intended to play everyone, but I knew I would have to bide my time to get a shot and there was still the prospect I might not get a game at all, depending on how the series played out. Ireland was bringing a strong squad led by the great Brian O'Driscoll, although they were at the end of an incredibly long season that had included the World Cup. It was the first time the Irish had played a three-test series here.

The series started incredibly well at a return to Eden Park for the first time since the World Cup final, highlighted by a hat-trick for my Hurricanes teammate Julian Savea in his first test and debuts for Aaron Smith and Brodie Retallick. It was a far different story in the second match in Christchurch where we were down to 14 players for the final eight minutes and survived an Irish onslaught as DC kicked a late drop goal to win it 22–19.

We'd been given the teaser that everyone should expect to play in the series and get some game time, but I was still waiting. I'd sat in all the strategy meetings where names are rarely used when describing moves, and every so often Steve would drop in a line like 'So, Beauds, you're going to be here . . .', but I'd roll my eyes and laugh it off. Often if you miss selection you will catch up with a coach later in the week and they may give you some idea of where you're placed for the next match, but heading into the third week of the Ireland series in Hamilton I was on tenterhooks. Sam Cane had made his debut in test two, leaving Luke Romano, Ben Tameifuna

My first test programme, against Ireland in 2012.

and me as the only newcomers who'd yet to play. We'd wrapped up the series, they'd said everyone would play . . . surely I was a chance?

As it turned out, the opportunity would have come regardless, as DC went down injured on the Tuesday beforehand, which is the day we find out the team. It's usually announced publicly on Thursday and there's a bit of a phoney war with the media as they try to figure out who's playing and we try to hide it, but in this case there wasn't much to hide — Aaron was starting and I was named on the bench for what would be my first test. I was relatively relaxed during the week, learning my role, and I felt excited about what was ahead, but what was keeping me up at night and giving me the most worry was trying to perfect the haka.

We do practise the haka, be it 'Ka Mate' or 'Kapa O Pango', and as there were so many new caps in the squad a lot of us were learning it during that series. Julian, Brodie and Aaron had needed to pick it up quickly, but Luke, who was starting in Hamilton, and I had a little more time and got in a few more practice sessions. While learning the movements and words is obviously important, understanding its meaning and significance and being able to convey that is just as vital. I was so worried about looking like a fool or coming across as disrespectful that on the team bus on the way to the stadium I watched videos of 'Ka Mate' on YouTube!

With that anxiety, I didn't fully get into the national anthem when we lined up at Waikato Stadium. Yes, I was proud as punch and all my family were in the crowd, but in the back of my mind I was thinking, 'I've got three games to play here — don't blow out on the first one, the anthem, nail the second one, the haka, and then try to enjoy the rest of it.' I got through it, tucked in the back (where I'd stay for many years), and remember a feeling of relief that I could now get on with the game.

Being on the bench is a unique position as you're never really sure if or when you'll get on and in what scenario. The forwards often have more of a clear plan because they have to learn the lineout moves in different positions, but for the backs it's a matter of watching and waiting. Whenever someone in my position would go down injured my heart rate would jump. After sitting back and enjoying a scintillating start by the team, that's exactly what happened that night.

Aaron had had a storming start to the game, carving up with Sonny Bill Williams through the middle, but after 25 minutes he took a knock in setting up the fourth try. On one hand, I was willing him to get up and be okay, but the other part of me was desperate to get out there. I was watching the managers talking through a microphone to the coaches, who at the same time were communicating with the medical staff, all the while keeping an eye on Aaron.

He was off and I was on. With the number 21 on my back, I ran on to Waikato Stadium as All Black number 1115. It wasn't just for a cameo at the end either but for 65 minutes of test rugby, driving a team around that was firing and leading 26-nil. It was an ideal scenario and I got an armchair ride, kicked a penalty from the sideline just before halftime for my first test points and basically had a blast. We scored another five tries in the second half and won it 60-nil, a record winning margin against Ireland.

Truth be told, though, the only reason I know any of this is because I've read the match report and stats. It was a blur. I've seen a few clips, but I've never watched the entire game back . . . if I hadn't looked at the match report I would have told you I'd played about 30 minutes in the second half, not three-quarters of the game!

One other thing that does stick with me from that night was swapping jerseys with Ireland's great first-five Ronan O'Gara, who'd also come off the bench. When I offered him mine he said, 'No, no, no. It's your first one. You keep it,' which was such a nice touch from a player I greatly admired and enjoyed watching play. That jersey is now back home at Mum and Dad's farm.

I might not remember much about the actual game, but just like my debut for Taranaki two years earlier, I was completely energised

Running into trouble in the form of big Munster man Peter O'Mahony during my first test match, Hamilton, 2012 . . .

afterwards. During a match, although you feel the energy, nerves and excitement of the crowd and it sometimes becomes frantic, everything going on in the stadium is almost like white noise in the background. We do feed off the crowd and having everyone on your side is empowering; you only need to hear the singing and chanting in places like Argentina or France, or see 'the Zoo' pumping in Dunedin, to work out the influence a crowd can have, but it's rare for me to be able to get a real gauge on the atmosphere. But once it's done — that's when you can soak up the moment.

There is great excitement after a test debut, but it's really the simplest pleasures after a game that are most enjoyable: a beer with your teammates and coaches in the changing sheds. You train so hard for a campaign, or a week, or a single game that sitting in the shed is the time to absorb your

. . . and clearly coming off second best. Others in the picture are Owen Franks and Ireland flanker Seán O'Brien.

success; it's the camaraderie of rugby, a small moment with your friends to reflect on what you've achieved regardless of what level you play.

Looking around the sheds that night, I felt immense pride and there was already a very tight bond forming between those of us who'd made their debuts in that series. Brodie, Sam and I had already had a big 12 months playing together and winning the under-20 World Cup the previous year, Aaron Smith had had a brilliant first series as the starting halfback in all three tests, and Dane Coles would come into the squad later that season. Between us we felt we could be among the next generation of leaders one day and when we would look at the honours board in the future, we wanted to see long lists of success next to our names over many years.

GETTY IMAGES

GETTY IMAGES

It's all over in Hamilton and I celebrate our win with Sam Cane.

Every rugby player who gets there knows that being an All Black is a big deal, but when those senior players speak in a huddle, at training or in a game, and they make eye contact with you, that's when you really feel it: the history, the expectation, the privilege. There's no bad time to learn, but to come into the All Blacks with the likes of Richie, Dan, Conrad and Keven Mealamu at the peak of their powers really was a golden moment. They were hugely influential and the newcomers were like sponges . . . partly because we were too scared to say anything, but mainly because we wanted to learn and were keen to stay in the team. I loved being there so much that I knew I never wanted to miss selection in another All Blacks squad for as long as possible. There were so many world-class players in the squad that every operating group like the front-rowers, loosies or midfield had at least one player who's now described as a legend of All Blacks rugby.

When legends of the game talk, they are putting themselves on the line and being vulnerable. As a young player that can make you uncomfortable, but it shows you how to grow, develop and be better. That's what you aspire to and what being an All Black is all about.

OPPOSITE: The All Blacks scored 60 points against the Irish in my debut test in Hamilton — I was happy to contribute with three conversions and a penalty goal.

View from the grandstand

by ROBYN BARRETT

When Beaudy called us to say he was going to be named on the bench for the third test against Ireland we were in a state of disbelief. It's not that we had any doubt in his ability, and we'd hoped it might happen that week, but for it to become reality was quite overwhelming. His selection was such a joyous moment for all of us and it was an incredibly special chapter in our life, but it meant that the rest of the week leading up to the match was a write-off. We were in la-la land and didn't achieve anything productive as we were so excited to share the news with family and close friends.

We experienced a full range of emotions during the week. Our family was flooded with beautiful, kind messages but there was also a level of anxiety that is quite unique to any parents; you only ever want the best for your kids and to protect them, so we also had to have a realistic understanding that things don't always play out as planned. The media interest was unreal and I had to stop listening to talkback radio and reading too many articles because I found the heartless, ill-informed knockers and the agenda of journalists hard to hear; negativity can take the gloss off a wonderful achievement which should be about celebration and enjoyment. Even now I'm still learning to ignore it and not to take opinions to heart — something which is very hard for a mum to do!

During the week we couldn't wait to get a wee message or phone call from Beaudy to hear about what was going on in the camp and get answers to our many questions . . . What was on the dinner menu? Who did you sit next to on the bus? Who are you rooming with? Did your goals go over in practice? Did Steve Hansen say much to you? It was so novel and exciting for us, so I can only imagine what was going through his mind.

It's about a four-hour drive from our farm in Taranaki to Hamilton, and in typical Barrett style — well, in typical Robyn and Kevin style I should say — we tried to cram plenty into test day and were late getting to the ground. Smiley wanted to duck into an Irish pub for 'a quick pint' and catch-up with a mate, so I was a bit grumpy as I could hear the national anthem playing just as we'd managed to get through the bag check at the security gates.

We plonked into our seats in time to see our skinny little son hiding away in the back of the haka, and all the emotions I'd experienced throughout the week hit me in one big go. Having tried to maintain the perspective that things might not play out in a certain way and there was a chance he may not even get on, there was no way we thought Beaudy would get the amount of game time he did. As he ran on after 25 minutes, I remember looking at Kevin and we were both shaking quite uncontrollably, and then it was an incredible feeling when he stepped up and slotted a goal from the sideline straight away.

With having such sporty kids, we'd always been mindful of never becoming pushy parents and putting unnecessary pressure on them. We tried to foster their love of sport, encouraged them to work hard, to make the most of the talent they'd been blessed with in all aspects of their lives, and to accept whatever occurred with grace and humility. To watch our son become an All Black was an immensely proud moment for us.

It was a momentous occasion and a day our whole family will never forget.

Teammates: 10 of the best

This could be a very dangerous game to play. Picking 'Dream Teams' or 'Greatest Players' lists is always a difficult decision-making process and I'm probably setting myself up to cop it from friends and teammates, both current and former!

Instead of a 'Best XV', I'm taking a different approach; this isn't necessarily a list of the greatest players to have laced a boot, but rather those I've enjoyed playing alongside at different levels and in a variety of teams. They are great teammates, friends and people who've had an influence on my career and who I admire; guys who have been a huge support to me, particularly as I came through the grades.

I've also taken a bit of iicence with the time frame as well. While the pages of this book have covered the early stages of my rugby life, only going as far as my first test in 2012, I've included a couple of others who I've played with in more recent times or who came into teams slightly later than I did but who are around the same age or stage of their careers.

GETTY IMAGES

1 KANE, SCOTT AND JORDIE BARRETT

Okay, it's possible I've cheated straight away by having three in one, but playing with my brothers is the ultimate.

Being the closet in age, Kane and I have played in many teams together. He was such an aggressive and versatile flanker-lock, captained Taranaki and played for the Blues before retiring aged 24 due to concussion. He's still heavily involved in rugby, coaching Coastal.

Jordie is the only one I've played with at Super Rugby level, making his Hurricanes debut in 2017 — not bad for the pesky little brother! Scott was a late bloomer, having to wait until year 13 to get a real crack at the First XV, but he has thrived in Canterbury and, like Kane, has shown his versatility and leadership ability. Scott, Jordie and I were the first trio of brothers to play in the same test for the All Blacks when we all turned out against Samoa in 2017.

I can't wait to play with Blake! He's a loose forward who has also captained Coastal and Dad reckons he's the toughest of the lot of us.

GETTY IMAGES

2 KURT BAKER

Kurt was alongside me for some of the most memorable moments in my early days: the national sevens in Queenstown, which led to selection in the New Zealand squad and my two tournaments in London and Edinburgh. He joined Taranaki from Manawatu in 2010, so we spent a lot of time playing together in the Amber and Blacks in 2010–11; his first game was also my debut against Northland.

Kurt has gone on to have a stellar career with the New Zealand Sevens team, winning two Commonwealth Games gold medals and two World Cups, scoring more than 100 tries on the world series, where he's become known for his double-thumbs up and other 'inventive' celebrations.

He's the ultimate team man, a real character and a bit of a clown!

GETTY IMAGES

3 BEN MAY

Ben is an old-school prop who is brutally honest! My old house mate in the early Hurricanes days, Ben is originally from a small town like me and eventually found his way to the big smoke. He joined the Canes in 2012 after making his debut for the Crusaders and playing for the Chiefs as well and has now played more than 100 Super Rugby games. He has also turned out in many campaigns in the Māori All Blacks.

Ben's versatility offers so much to a team as he can play both sides of the scrum and always makes an impact whether he starts or comes off the bench. He's always a popular team man.

GETTY IMAGES

4 ISRAEL DAGG

Not afraid of throwing in a goosestep, Izzy had brilliant instincts as a fullback and dazzling footwork. He lit up the 2011 World Cup, scoring the opening try of the tournament, and had a big hand in the All Blacks' success in that campaign. Izzy was at fullback and scored a try in my test debut against Ireland in 2012. It's easy to forget that he was actually with the Highlanders when he was first picked for the All Blacks in 2010 because he was such a big part of the Crusaders' dominance. Izzy played 66 tests and should be considered among the most outstanding fullbacks to play the game; it's such a shame he was forced to retire early because of a knee injury. But most of all he's a great mate, excellent golf buddy and someone you can always count on for a laugh. Izzy had a great perspective about life as a professional rugby player.

GETTY IMAGES

5 JAMES MARSHALL

I played with James at both Taranaki and the Hurricanes and we spent hours together plotting, strategising and devising attack plans. He's such a versatile back, mainly first-five or fullback, but he has been known to slot in on the wing and at 12 as well. He's played in Italy, England and Japan, so has experienced many different types of rugby. James was part of the Hurricanes when we won the Super Rugby title in 2016. The fact that James was named Hurricanes 'team man of the year' more than three times tells you so much about what a great person and teammate he is. He's a genuine comedian and loves a punt!

GETTY IMAGES

6 DANE COLES

Don't tell anyone this, but deep down Dane Coles is just a big softy.

He made his test debut on the end-of-year tour in 2012, just a few months after I'd played my first test. He's among that group with Sam Cane, Aaron Smith, Brodie Retallick and others who came into the All Blacks at around the same time and thought we could be the next group to carry on the work of the likes of Richie, Dan and Conrad.

A ball-running hooker like no other, Colesy was the captain when the Hurricanes won Super Rugby. It has been impressive to watch him fight back from injuries and battle through those tough times. He's a bit rough around the edges but he's a great man and I loved winding him up on a daily basis when we were at the Canes together.

GETTY IMAGES

7 DAMIAN MCKENZIE

My successful midweek golfing partner, Damian is so exciting to watch on the rugby field. If I'm not playing, I always like to keep an eye on what my All Blacks teammates are doing in Super Rugby and get a real thrill watching them achieve. Damian is small but he's so explosive and fearless, brilliant in the air and makes the fans get out of their seats. He was a bit of a star at schoolboy level a few years ago and made a big call to move up north to the Waikato despite being from Southland, but he has gone from strength to strength at the Chiefs. It was such a blow to lose him to injury before the 2019 World Cup. He's an all-round great man.

GETTY IMAGES

8 ANTON LIENERT-BROWN

Another of the golfing gang. Anton's career has actually followed a very similar trajectory to Damian's; they are both South Islanders who were really talented schoolboys, moved to the Chiefs and made their test debuts within a few months of each other. I'll leave it up to them to argue over who is the better golfer.

Anton is one of those rare players who made his Super Rugby debut before he'd played provincial rugby. I was playing inside Anton when he made his test debut against Australia in 2016 in Wellington and he had a storming game. He's such an assured midfielder. I love the perspective he has on life and rugby. Anton is someone who I can always count on for a chat.

GETTY IMAGES

9 TJ PERENARA

TJ and I know each other inside out and we have played over 100 games together at the Hurricanes. TJ's debut for the Canes was off the bench against the Stormers in 2012, in what was also my first start at Super Rugby level.

He came through the ranks in Wellington rugby so is a true product of the Hurricanes' system and he has rewarded the region 10 times over with his passion and commitment, becoming the most capped Canes player. He had to bide his time for an All Blacks debut but is a player who makes the most of every opportunity and it's amazing to have seen him grow into a great leader on and off the field.

TJ is a fierce competitor who would always keep me on my toes!

JOHN VELVIN/ESPNZ

10 RICK MCKENNA

Rick was a teammate at Francis Douglas Memorial College and the Coastal club. A talented first-five, he played in the New Zealand Schools team with my brother Kane. He has played more than 100 games for Coastal and has been a bit of a points-scoring machine in club rugby. Rugby has taken Rick around the world, with stints in the UK and Ireland, and a couple of games for Taranaki.

He was a cheeky lad who had a great bag of rugby balls and we spent hours kicking together.

FALKE

CHAPTER 5
Skills & drills

It all starts with the basics. For me, it began with Dad's lessons on the farm and his three key points that were drummed into us:

- Ball in two hands.
- Kick off both feet.
- Pass both ways.

Dad was really big on teaching us how important it was to be able to use both sides. He would often remind us: 'If you have the ball under one arm, it's obvious you are going to run, *but* as soon as the ball is in two hands you'll have your opponent guessing what you're going to do.' Dad coached some of my and my brothers' teams through primary school and would drum the basics into us, ask us what we'd noticed about the All Blacks game on the weekend and make sure we were having fun throwing the ball around or using him for tackling practice.

They are three really simple things to keep in mind when you are practising your different skills, but it will take time to develop the ability to pass both ways and kick off both feet because it will feel a bit unnatural. There's a real thrill, though, in seeing improvement, trying and sometimes failing, trying again and again and then mastering a skill.

Hopefully, you're playing lots of different sports, so think about how they can help your rugby. A sport like cricket is a team game, but the skills are very individualised and that is an idea I like to bring to my rugby practice at home or whenever I'm not with my teammates; passing is one skillset, kicking is another, being fit and fast another. Rugby, like other sports, has a lot of individual elements so the training you do by yourself also helps the team.

There's truly only one way to get better: practise! When I was younger, I would spend hours outside because we were playing many different games and having lots of different competitions, but I also now like a 'little and often' approach: doing short sessions regularly. Regular and consistent practice is the key to mastering each skill, and once you think

you've nailed something, practise it some more so it becomes second nature to your brain and your muscles.

There are many things in a game that you can't control, such as the weather, the opposition, the crowd or whether your mum is being a bit embarrassing with her cheering on the sidelines. What you can control, however, is how much practice you put into improving before you get to game day. You will have lots of different coaches who may each have a different style or ideas, but the principles of all rugby skills stay the same so it's important to listen to what your coach says and ask any questions you have. Remember too that when it comes to game time it's okay to be nervous. In fact, I think nerves are a good thing because it means you won't take your opposition lightly and you have respect for them.

Warming up

Don't forget to warm up. A quick 5 to 10-minute warm-up will not only prevent injury but will help you with rotation and flexibility, resulting in a more productive and rewarding training session.

Here are some simple warm-up exercises:

- A quick 100-metre jog with side strides followed by leg swings while holding the goalposts. This will loosen up your legs.
- Lunges with a twist over your front leg to get into the hips, and calf pumps to stretch out those lower legs — you should be starting to feel warm.
- Lying on your back, bring your knee up and across your body to loosen up your lower back.
- Do some 10-metre shuttles; then butt kicks and high knees to get those muscles firing.
- Throw in some gradual 20-metre sprints with footwork to practise your evasion.
- You should be ready to get into some shorter kicks to get your kicking or training session going.
- If you're heading into some contact drills you need to prime yourself for this — warming up with press-ups, pummelling with a partner and even wrestling on your knees is a good way to get yourself ready.

Most importantly, playing and practising for rugby should be fun so make sure you enjoy yourself!

Tackling

First things first — don't forget to put your mouth guard in! You should have one in for practice anyway, but certainly when you are practising tackling it's a must because one of the most important things here is safety.

Having good tackle technique is vital to keep both you and your opponent safe, to stop the ball carrier in their tracks, get them to ground and hopefully help your team win a turnover. Even if you are small, you can still be an effective tackler if you have the right technique and determination.

There are two main types of tackles: **front on** and **side on**.

When tackling from front on you will want to be looking at your opponent's hips as they come towards you.

REMEMBER: Safety is paramount — if you're looking at their hips, your head will be in a good position.

Your footwork going into contact needs to be quick and reactive to what the attacking player is doing in order to get into a strong position with light feet and your weight on your toes. If you're tackling on your right, your right leg will be going forward with your right shoulder making contact, and vice versa for the left side, as you dip your body late towards your opponent, aiming to make contact under the ball. Remember here to still keep your eyes on your opponent's hips.

TIP:
Always keep your eyes open and your feet moving to get in the best position to make a good tackle. Never look at the opponent's feet, especially if they're a good stepper.

As you make the tackle your head should be to the side and you're looking to punch your arm around your opponent's body and wrap the arms strongly around them.

Drive through the tackle with your legs; this is so important if you want to make a dominant tackle.

You are aiming to end up on top of your opponent, in the dominant position. This allows you to roll away or get up quickly and be ready for the next play.

Many of the principles for a *side-on* tackle are the same as for a front-on one, but there are a couple of key things to remember.

Use the sideline to give the attacker only one option, one side of the field to go towards, remembering to keep your eyes on their hips as you shepherd them sideways.

Keeping your body nice and low as you dip into the tackle, you're aiming here for 'cheek-to-cheek' contact — i.e. your ear against their butt.

Once again, a nice strong wrap of the arms around the attacker's thighs or legs will help you drive the tackle and finish in a position to swing up off the ground and contest the ball at the breakdown.

Catch-pass

Of all the fundamentals of rugby, catching and passing is the most important, and is something you can practise without even really being conscious you're doing so. In today's game every player from number one to number 23 needs to be able to pass the ball. Even the big forwards require a good short-passing game to manipulate defences with their running lines and put their teammate through a small seam or crack in the defensive line. You don't always have to throw a spiral and, in particular, end-over-end shorter passes are easier to catch. However, as a back or if you're in open space, a bullet spiral pass is the fastest way to spread the ball.

Before you pass the ball, you have to catch it! Get your hands up nice and early to receive the pass with the aim of catching it slightly away from your body so that it doesn't hit you on the chest and bobble out. Let your slightly bent arms and fingers absorb the impact of the ball. An early catch gives you more time with the ball to make the right decision.

Hand position on ball — using your fingers, thumbs and wrists you will generate spin on the ball. Most of the spin will come from your top hand rotating over the ball towards your body.

With your hands in good position, loaded and ready to generate spin, simultaneously rotate your upper body and punch your arms across the body. Punch your arms towards the target to maximise your power from your upper body and triceps.

The ball will go where your hands are aiming, so follow through the pass with your fingers and hands pointing towards the target.

TIP:
Practise off both sides. One way to do this by yourself is to spin the ball upwards into the air from each side, right to left and left to right, to get used to the movement, then you can practise passing to a friend or parent, or even against a wall. It may seem difficult and quite unnatural at first, but you'll master it in no time.

PRACTISE:
Catching and passing while running in a straight line. This is the best way to expand and grow your vision, as well as to open yourself up for more running opportunities.

High-ball catch

One of the most difficult catches to make is taking a high ball, but when done right it looks spectacular, gets the crowd on its feet and is lots of fun to practise. There are a lot of factors to consider when trying to take a high ball, such as what the wind is doing and the height and trajectory of the ball, while trying not to worry about the opposition coming at you. It's always vital, but if ever there was a skill to remember to keep your eye on the ball for, this is it!

As the ball goes up you need to run towards it, coming at it from a bit of an angle, so rather than running at it in a straight line you want to run forwards in a slight curve. This is where you will need to judge if you need to really accelerate or take smaller steps to adjust.

Keep moving towards the ball as it's coming down; you want to be jumping FORWARDS and UP on that angle. It's important to avoid being stationary underneath it as it is easier to catch the ball if you are running and jumping into the contest. If you are standing still as you take the ball, it's much more likely you'll get pummelled by the oncoming defenders!

As you go up for the ball, your knee should be high, elbows tucked in and with your body slightly turned away from the opposition. Use your chest to support the ball as you make the catch.

As you make the catch and are on your way back down, lock your body into a strong brace position (above left). Keeping your body nice and compact will help you absorb and protect yourself from the opponent in the air or from the defenders and contact as you land (above right). Remember to keep that body on an angle — if you are facing forward, that's where the ball will go if you drop it and this exposes your body to a big hit!

Kicking

There are many different styles and tactical uses for the variety of kicks in the game. As my dad always says, learning to kick off both feet can be a real asset to the team and a great string to your bow, giving you options for whatever scenario you find yourself in.

DROP PUNT

This is the most common way to kick for touch or downfield, trying to turn your opposition around and put your team in a good attacking position. To start with, use the sideline and 5-metre line as a channel to work in and aim to kick 15 to 20 metres downfield.

Place two hands on the ball. The ball should be perpendicular to the ground, so it looks upright not on its side.

Jog slowly in a straight line, taking short steps to stay balanced and controlled as you prepare to release it.

With the ball still in that upright position, release the ball around waist height in line with your kicking leg. If you are right-handed/footed, use your right hand to guide it and vice versa for lefties.

As you are making contact with the ball, your foot should be firm, hard and pointed, and looking for the bottom of the ball to hit your bootlaces.

Stand tall and keep your posture upright so that you stay balanced as your leg keeps moving through.

As the ball has left the boot, let the leg swing through and keep jogging a few steps towards the target, which will encourage you to get all your weight and energy going in the correct direction.

TIP:
To get more distance, follow the same principles but approach the kick on a small 45-degree angle or curve, which will mean your leg can flex further back and allow you to wind into the kick. If you want to kick the ball high, follow the same principles but lean slightly back to allow your follow-through to be more 'up' rather than 'along'.

PRACTISE:
As you develop a nice, consistent strike and ball flight, see if you can repeat this *but land on your kicking foot.* This is how you kick those flat cross-field kick-passes to the wing. An upright posture is critical in order to strike these low and hard (don't lean back).

DROP-KICK

There are two uses for drop-kicks — for goal or for restarts — and the principles are similar for both. But there's a big difference in that a restart is very controlled, whereas if you are trying to drop-kick for points there are many variables: how far from the posts, how the pass comes at you, defenders rushing forward and what stage the game is in. It can be a pressure kick, but it can also be a match-winning one!

Just as when you are trying to get more distance with a drop punt, prepare to make your drop-kick on a 45-degree angle, taking small steps forward.

Drop the ball upright in front of your crotch, aiming to have the nose of the ball pointed towards your own nose.

The aim is to smother the ball (above) and not give it too much time to pop up, where you might lose control of it (top right & right). You want to move your leg through quickly and make contact with the ball soon after the bounce; the sooner you connect with it, the longer and flatter it will fly. As the ball has left the boot, let the leg swing through and keep jogging a few steps towards the target, which will encourage you to get all your weight and energy going in the correct direction.

Follow through with your kicking leg. Finish balanced and square; your body and chest should be in line with the target.

PRACTISE:
Try drop-kicking for goal from different positions on the field and distances on the posts. Ask a friend or parent to pass the ball at different heights so you can practise the adjustments you might need to make in a game situation.

TIP:
If you are drop-kicking to restart the game, lean back a little as you swing through and wait for the ball to pop a bit higher. You should feel your leg and the ball going 'up' instead of 'along'.

GOAL-KICKING

Goal-kicking practice should always be fun, and it's so easy to see and measure success. Hopefully, that enjoyment will translate into a game and help take away any nerves. Any time I have an important kick I stick to the exact same process as I would do on the training field and remember to do it with a smile, although I keep my smile inside me rather than the grin you actually see on Damian McKenzie's face when he kicks. I love kicking goals.

There are many ways to do it and no 'right' way. The height of your tee and how you place the ball on it is your personal preference, as is how many steps back you take and the routine you go through (breathing, smiling, finger wiggles etc.). I used a high tee for a long time and now prefer a lower tee, so things can change and it's really about what you feel most comfortable with. You will find your natural technique and what suits you, but whatever the routine, it needs to be simple and consistent.

Place ball on tee (left low tee, right high tee). Use the seam of the ball to line up correctly to the target.

Take your chosen number of steps back (I take five) and breathe to focus on the task at hand. This is where you want to be calm and relaxed. Blocking out external noise can be a challenge, but it's something you can work on occasionally with mates distracting you. You need to be consistent with this process!

Watching the back of the ball, stay tall and upright as you approach it with control. You want to feel light and balanced as you prepare for the final two steps, which are the most important.

Your plant foot (or non-kicking foot) should be in line with the tee and pointing towards the target. You need to give yourself room to swing your kicking leg through without losing balance, so your plant foot shouldn't be too close to the tee.

When you make contact with the ball your foot should be firm as you accelerate through and beyond the ball (above left). If you are using a low tee, make contact with the lower third of the ball (above centre), but if you have a high tee it will be right at the bottom (above right).

Your kicking leg and body should follow through towards the target.

TIP: Practise kicking at various stages of a training session — it's easier to kick a goal if you've watched the forwards score a try from a rolling maul than if you've just run 80 metres or it's the 79th minute of the game when your legs are tired. It's important to practise kicking while you are feeling fatigued just as much as when you're fresh — remember to keep the process and flow the same every time.

REMEMBER: Your technique may change or need adjusting slightly as your body changes and grows.

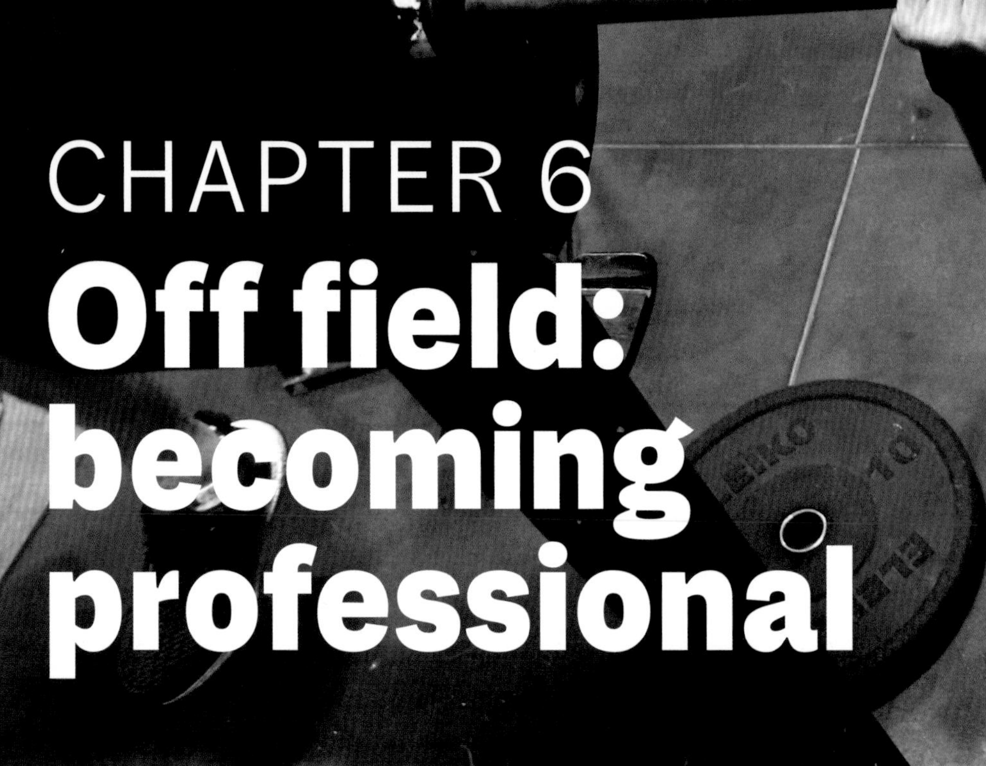

CHAPTER 6
Off field: becoming professional

GETTY IMAGES

When I was growing up, I never thought higher honours were realistic because I was quite small and not overly strong or fast. I hardly had the physical stature of a professional rugby player. But the beauty of the game is that there's a place for all shapes and sizes and ways to overcome that perception of 'not being big enough'. It can, however, take time.

Back when my skinny legs and big ears earnt me the nickname Rabbit, I used to run everywhere. Our teachers at Pungarehu primary school would send us for runs around the block most days to burn off some energy, and Mum would encourage us to run home from school and try to beat the bus. It was about four kilometres down Lower Parihaka Road and we were always in bare feet; in fact, I don't think I wore a pair of shoes, aside from when we were in Ireland, until I went to high school.

We were all heavily into athletics, and when I was 12 years old I went to Auckland for the Colgate Games, the track and field event for kids

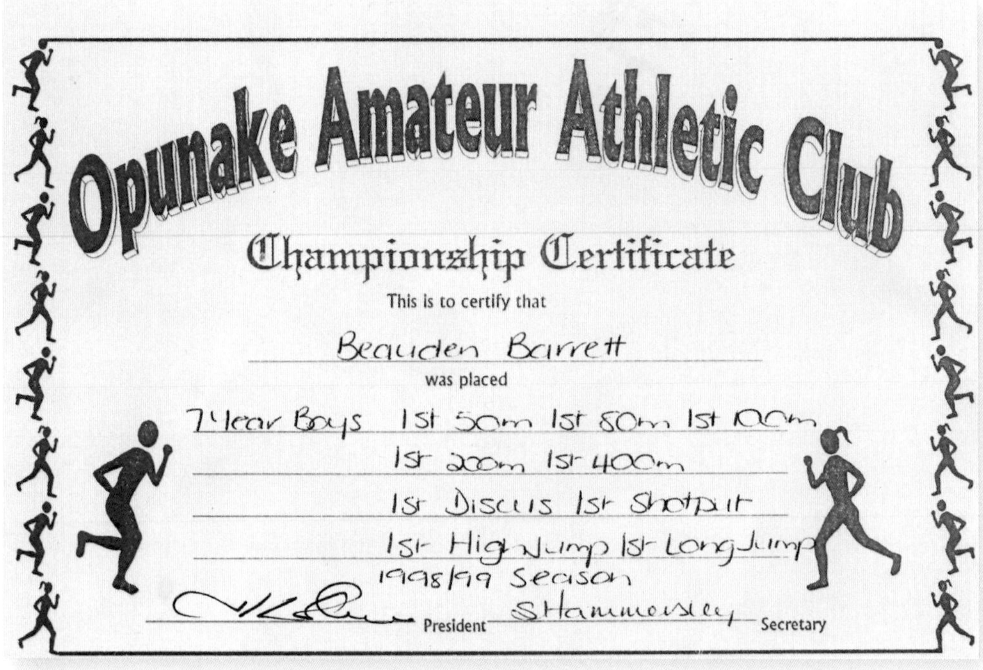
Opunake Amateur Athletic Club

Championship Certificate

This is to certify that

Beauden Barrett

was placed

7 Year Boys 1st 50m 1st 80m 1st 100m
1st 200m 1st 400m
1st Discus 1st Shotput
1st High Jump 1st Long Jump
1998/99 Season

President S Hammersley Secretary

Athletics were a big part of my early life — this certificate was awarded in the Opunake AAC 7 Year Boys category during the 1998–1999 season.

aged from about seven through to 14 that has been running for more than 40 years. I competed in most of the running and jumping events, and it was here I had a rude awakening as to where my natural talent lay at the time. Lining up across the track for the 200 metres sprint was a guy from Auckland who I thought was an official as he was way too big to be a kid competing. I was wrong, and as I watched Ben Lam scorch everyone in the sprint events, I decided I was probably best to focus on middle-distance running and long-range fitness and ended up having good success in the 3–5k events as a junior, while Ben went on to be a sprint star throughout high school and at a national level.

Running on the flat was boring, so I'd love nothing better than long barefoot runs around the farm, up and down hills, hurdling electric fences along the way. All that running combined with the other sports I played meant I was always fit. It wasn't something I necessarily had to work on but was something I wanted to continually improve upon; I was never

BARRETT FAMILY COLLECTION

Lining up as a 12-year-old in the 200 metres event at the Colgate Games in Auckland. That's me in the yellow and green uniform, second from the outside.

satisfied; I wanted to be fitter and fitter. As rugby became more serious through the Taranaki rep grades and First XV, the way I saw it there's always a point in every game where you'd feel tired, so I wanted that feeling to come later than everyone else and have a higher threshold. Because I didn't really develop any speed until I properly started weight training aged 18 and couldn't offer much in the way of size, fitness was one of my weapons against bigger, faster players.

Perhaps one reason I was small and thin, particularly compared to my brothers Kane and Scott, was that they were quite good, healthy eaters and I was a sweet tooth (still am) who loved a treat. They also went via the fridge when we got home from school before heading out to play, whereas I was back out the door as soon as my schoolbag had been dropped inside. It became apparent when I was around 15 and going into First XV rugby that I would need to eat more and put on weight to be able to compete with the bigger boys since there can be quite a difference between a year 11 and year 13 player. Being at boarding school, I had to drink a lot of milk and eat copious amounts of toast for snacks or supper in a desperate attempt to gain some mass.

As Davie Gray discovered when I arrived at the Hurricanes, my physique was still very much a work in progress. My complete lack of cooking skills probably didn't help with the seemingly never-ending quest to put on weight in the early days of my career. Mum was such a great cook and I went to boarding school during the week, so I didn't have to get my own meals until I moved to Wellington, where it became obvious that I was a total liability in the kitchen. My first year I lived with Tyson Keats and James Broadhurst on Tory Street, just off Courtenay Place, so whenever it was my turn to cook we'd generally eat out. Things didn't really improve when I moved into Jason Eaton's place with James, Richard Buckman and Ben May, where the most stressful, strenuous part of the week would often be my painstaking efforts at cooking a roast chicken or chicken burritos, my two go-to dishes. It wasn't until I met

When I first started out in professional rugby, I hated the gym. Now, it's just part of life.

Hannah, my now wife, that I learned to cook thanks to her lessons!

It meant that to get the weight gains that Davie and nutritionists at the Hurricanes wanted to see was, at times, a bit of a chore. I was pretty much constantly stuffing my face, which isn't nearly as fun as it sounds, and in sticking to the portion sizes they wanted I'd often turn up to afternoon training sessions feeling bloated and nauseous. I prefer to run around on an empty stomach, so if you can imagine you've just eaten a massive, delicious dinner and dessert, the kind that puts you into a food coma, and then you have to go for a run — that was me most days. Rather than a big plate of food, I found it better to get the calories in one go with a smoothie and then would top up with snacks. But more often than not, I would feel physically uncomfortable with it all sloshing around my stomach.

I also hated the gym. Hated it! Davie knew I did and I think he got some enjoyment out of that but also realised we had to channel that dislike and find a way to get through it if I was going to continue to see

GETTY IMAGES

More weights, more food, more training helped me progress quickly.

improvements. Listening to good music was a big factor, as was the ability to modify the programme to do more of the lifts and exercises I preferred rather than sticking with the same reps over and over. On an average rugby week, if I'm playing on a Saturday, I'd usually have two or three weight sessions, but I was doing five, waking up every day with sore muscles and having to go again. I also set myself back at times by going out drinking on the weekends and not being able to eat properly the next day. Early in my Hurricanes career I sometimes dreaded it: more weights, more food, more training, and it felt never-ending but was critical in helping me progress quickly.

Having that extra size gave me a heap more confidence, knowing I could attack the line and not get cleaned up every single time. I didn't have the physique of someone like Damian McKenzie, who while small and light is very explosive; I was a beanpole, skinny and gangly, so to have more mass around my shoulders and chest and extra weight gave me confidence that my body could handle what was coming. Yes, there were and are still times where I meet my match and get knocked back as fast as I run it up, but there's a big difference between the 78 kilos I was in my final year of school to the 88 kg I was at for my test debut three years later and to the 93 kg that I play at now. It's a gradual process and important to do it with the right advice.

Things like eating well, maintaining fitness when a trainer isn't standing over you barking orders and looking after yourself are part of the largely unseen side of being a sportsperson. So is the homework.

There's a lot that goes on behind the scenes, with little rugby conversations constantly taking place in the classroom, at strategy meetings or in mini-unit meetings, where each positional group (inside backs, loosies, front row . . .) gets together. I have used a notebook every season since starting out with Taranaki and I'm detailed in my note-taking. Each week I'll write out attacking ideas for me and the team, or the coaches will set us tasks to look at different elements of the game and from there we come up with a clear strategy, depending on who we're playing. For me, a lot of it is based around attack, but the notebooks also have defensive plans and the systems a team uses. Each team has different names for every skill, move or element, so when playing for multiple teams in a season, like 2011 when I played for the Canes, under-20s and the Naki, there's a lot to remember . . . and a lot of notebooks.

A coach might ask for attacking ideas for a specific scenario, so I can delve back into them to try to find something that might work. While the game constantly changes, there are times when you can pull out classic moves that work a treat; when I started in Super Rugby, Alama Ieremia had a move called 'Canes 97', one he'd used as a player and which we tried 15 years later to score with against the Chiefs. There's a lot for a first-five to think about, so towards the end of each week I like to simplify everything down to one page, drawn up like a rugby field with the moves and options written where they might be used.

Reviewing my training notes during a gym session.

Studying was never my strong suit at school. There's a real art to it regardless of what career path you're going down, but it's a good example of why note-taking and writing things down are so useful and an important part of rugby development. Over the years, I've used them as part of my personal planning as well: what a good training week looks like, how to review and tinker with things, what's working, what's not, how I was feeling at any given time and what I'd do differently. It's basically like a library and there's plenty of gold in those notebooks.

§

The other things those notebooks helped me with was finding my voice.

Every time you join a team there's new people to meet, teammates and coaches to connect with and, in my case early on, having to learn

GETTY IMAGES

With All Blacks coach Ian Foster . . . when I first joined them, he stressed the importance of 'selling' a good story to the team.

to get outside my comfort zone and be able to talk to and deliver the strategy to others.

From being nearly speechless while having lunch with Richie on my first day in All Blacks camp, I would soon have to stand in front of him and others to present various game plans. While I had gained confidence doing so with Taranaki and the Hurricanes, it's a different story when it's the best players in New Zealand and guys I'd looked up to for a long time. But they needed to hear my voice and I needed to be comfortable in myself and in what I was presenting; otherwise they wouldn't have any confidence in the new young guy to drive them around the park.

I did a lot of work on this initially with Ian Foster. Forwards are a funny bunch as it is, let alone when they're sitting together watching and waiting to hear what you've got for them. Fossie probably thought I was a good communicator anyway, but he impressed upon me the importance

GETTY IMAGES

of selling a good story to the team and getting the forwards to buy into it.

Fossie would first have to sell it to Steve Hansen and then we first-fives would walk through it on a Monday and maybe simplify it before presenting it to the squad. But you can't just roll up each week with the same presentations, so we use diagrams, illustrations and other creative ways to get the message across; the detail of the strategy and how you present it are almost 50–50 in terms of importance. Fossie is really good at it, very creative, and would be an excellent salesman.

A first-five has a lot on their shoulders and it can therefore take a long time to develop into the job, but it's a role and position I love. Maybe I'm a bit of a control freak, but I like to be the one making the decisions rather than waiting on someone else to do so. I enjoy calling the shots, influencing the team or a game and taking that responsibility. At 10, you have to know everything, all the calls and their names, everything that's on the 'menu' of options and scenarios, and be able to make the decision within a split second. Having added pressure is probably why I enjoy playing at 10 more than I do at fullback, which is much more instinctual and reaction based. Being able to play at the back does also help me to be a better first-five, giving me a different perspective on what the team needs from their pivot.

Versatility can be a blessing and a curse, but having understanding of other roles and positions is important, as is being a good bench player or team person if you're not in the game-day squad. It was only in my second years at both Taranaki and the Hurricanes that I gained a regular starting spot, and little did I know then that after my first All Blacks test off the bench it would be another two seasons and 20 tests before I'd get a chance to start.

Bench players have a clear role — make an impact and lift the starters

OPPOSITE: Learning to be a good bench player is vitally important to your team.

to a second wind, giving them energy when they might need it. For me it's about being everywhere, being busy, getting off the ground quickly to be in support and getting lots of touches on the ball. It can be a bit of a slippery slope for the forwards, who sometimes come on a bit too fired up and players who don't say a word at training are suddenly saying too much . . . they need a bit of calming down at times.

It's okay to be disappointed if you miss out on selection; it shows you care. But you may just have to put on a brave face, and then when you're by yourself can be the time to drop your lip a bit or call your parents and say you should be in the team. When I didn't play in the first two tests of that Ireland series, my priority was to do whatever I could to help Dan and Aaron be ready: passing balls, holding tackle bags, returning kicks and offering support in any way, shape or form while still developing and learning from two of the best. You can be hurting and still be able to suck it up and do what's best for the team . . . use that frustration to drive you so when it is your time and opportunity, you're ready to go.

OPPOSITE: When I don't make the run-on side, I always do my best to support the starting player. Here I am with former All Blacks great, Dan Carter.

Athletes: 10 of the best

I love most sports and enjoy watching the best in the world at what they do. When I was young, I watched a lot of cricket, particularly the Black Caps teams captained by Stephen Fleming, and in more recent times have avidly followed the teams of Brendon McCullum and Kane Williamson.

Most Saturday, Sunday and Monday mornings I can be found, where possible, watching golf. The time difference for the PGA Tour events and major golf championships in the USA means more than a few Monday mornings are glued to the TV!

You might see a bit of a theme then in my top 10 favourite athletes from other codes to watch — although I couldn't go past having an All Black from a previous generation in this list!

GETTY IMAGES

1 TIGER WOODS

Tiger changed the face of golf and indeed world sport. His career has had huge highs and some pretty massive lows, yet he's fought back more than once and his comeback to win the 2019 Masters was extraordinary.

GETTY IMAGES

2 MICHAEL JORDAN

Three of Michael Jordan's six NBA titles with the Chicago Bulls came when I was playing basketball as a little fella at primary school. Jordan, like Tiger, was a game changer in leading the explosion in the NBA's popularity around the world and many believe he is the greatest of all time.

GETTY IMAGES

3 RORY MCILROY

Won three major golf titles before he turned 25 and has stayed at the top for a long time, despite the pressure that comes with being so successful at such a young age. Rory's also a massive rugby fan and I was lucky to meet him and get a few golf tips from him!

GETTY IMAGES

4 ROGER FEDERER

Most sports fans and people who are into tennis sit in one of two camps: Roger or Rafa — I'm in the Roger Federer camp. His longevity and sustained excellence will be hard for any athlete in any sport to replicate, and to many he is the most elegant tennis player in history, let alone being the greatest to play the game in some minds.

GETTY IMAGES

5 RICKIE FOWLER

Rickie is one of the colourful, exciting new breed of golfers. He's full of talent and seems like he's enjoying himself most of the time he's on the course; he's entertaining to watch.

GETTY IMAGES

6 AB DE VILLIERS

Speaking of athletes who entertain, it's hard to go past AB de Villiers as one of the most explosive, exciting cricketers of the past generation to watch. I mean, a one-day century in just 31 balls is unbelievable and to have a batting average of more than 50 in both tests and one-day cricket is something few can do. Seeing AB stride to the crease would always make me expect to see something special.

GETTY IMAGES

7 ANDREW JOHNS

A brilliant ball player with a superb kicking game, Andrew Johns could more often than not win rugby league games single-handedly and carry teams on his shoulders. Some of the things he could do on the field were mind-blowing.

GETTY IMAGES

8 SACHIN TENDULKAR

The Little Master. Sachin Tendulkar is one of the sportspeople that in 20 years' time you will be grateful that you'll be able to tell young kids that you saw him play. He was such a prolific batsman it's impossible to single out any one thing he did over his international career, which lasted more than 20 years.

GETTY IMAGES

9 PHIL MICKELSON

Just one more golfer! Like me, Phil Mickelson is actually right-handed but plays golf left-handed, and he's seen to be the best 'leftie' to play the game. His rivalry with Tiger was also always enjoyable to watch.

GETTY IMAGES

10 CHRISTIAN CULLEN

I couldn't finish without having another rugby player on the list, one I didn't play with. Cully would probably make most people's rugby 'Dream Teams' or favourite player list because he was electric. He could glide through a gap with his beautiful balanced running style and speed.

• Electrical
• Security
adidas
AIG
ALL BLACKS
ALL BLACKS
select

CHAPTER 7
Goals and mind games

When you sign a contract to become a professional rugby player, there's no guidebook to show you how to navigate a way through it. There's an army of people that are part of the off-field support for every team: coaches, managers, nutritionists, trainers, personal development managers, doctors and physios who are all experts in their fields chosen to guide players and teams. But just like teachers or sports coaches at school, in many instances they can only provide guidance and advice. I had plenty of those people to help me, but ultimately I was the only one who could truly decide and control the player I wanted to be on the field and the person I wanted to be off it.

There's a reason guys like Richie McCaw, Kieran Read and Dan Carter played more than 100 tests for the All Blacks — they were never satisfied and never complacent, they knew they couldn't rely on their last performance because there was always another game around the corner that could whack them on the nose. In some cases you see a player sign a contract and think they've 'made it', when they haven't even started, haven't played a game. When a young player has dominated at secondary-school level, gets a big offer thrown at them and things have gone smoothly, there can be a danger that they think the job is done, but in reality it's when the hard work properly begins.

It's easy to see how professional sport can chew up a young player and spit them out. For me it all happened so quickly. New teams, new management, new teammates, moving from New Plymouth to Wellington, travelling around the country and then around the world, a Taranaki debut aged 19 and an All Blacks appearance at 21. At times it was a rollercoaster and I was clinging on for the ride; it was a lot of fun, but my head was spinning.

Those first couple of years living with the likes of Jason Eaton, James Broadhurst and Richard Buckman was such a fun time in all our lives. We were still learning how to be professional athletes and figuring out how to balance the social side with training and performing. Sometimes I got a bit too social and I'm probably lucky that I didn't get into really big trouble after a couple of nights out.

Steve Symonds, our personal development manager at the Hurricanes, was often the person I'd go to if things had taken a turn for the worse over the weekend. On one occasion in 2011, I was caught on the big screen at the Wellington Sevens in clearly not great shape, and while I was a new player that only the real rugby nuts would have recognised, the night certainly escalated and I was still worried about how it would look and was thinking the worst. I went to Steve and told him I'd had a bit of a blowout and I think that's still the best way, to front foot any issue or incident before it becomes a bigger deal or makes it into the media.

In late 2011 our Hurricanes coach Mark Hammett sat me down with Steve, wanting to discuss my drinking. He thought I had a problem and should move out of Jason's place. I was enjoying the weekends, but I certainly don't think I had or ever have had a problem with drinking. But from his perspective it was an issue for where he wanted me to be as a young player coming through.

It was a moment to take that advice on board and listen to how someone else was seeing me. I did end up buying my own place fairly soon after and changing things up a bit. I would give myself curfews or prioritise when the right time to have a night out was; certainly Davie Gray could tell what sort of weekend I'd had by the way I handled our first gym session of the week, and it didn't take long to realise how much better I felt with fewer nights out. Ultimately, it was being aware of not throwing away the opportunities I had, but also simply part of maturing and learning to be a pro athlete.

Steve Symonds has had a huge influence and helped me with some testing times as a young professional when those social issues and tricky situations came up. We first met at a Hurricanes Schools camp back in 2009 where he came to offer advice about going from high school into

The Hurricanes' Davie Gray, a master of physical performance.

the next phase of our lives, be it in rugby, going to university, taking up a trade or into the workforce.

When I joined the Canes in 2011, Steve and I clicked . . . even though I didn't enjoy some of the things he made us do. The new recruits and young players are given additional support, and because we all come from such diverse backgrounds everyone starts on the same entry level with some of the 'life skills' courses. While I was quite interested in financial planning, to sit through sessions with lawyers or accountants, media training, toastmasters or whatever else Steve had lined up for us wasn't always my favourite couple of hours each week. But he was always someone players could trust and go to for advice about legal or financial issues, uncertainty about handling a media situation and even contract negotiations. There were times when he had to tell me to pull my head in and he knew how to deliver a message that would get through to me, particularly around going out on the weekends.

While Steve cared about what I was doing on the field and how that side was developing, his primary focus was how I was as an individual

DAVE LINTOTT PHOTOGRAPHY

Steve Symonds, personal development manager at the Hurricanes, helped me through some testing times.

and in trying to find that life balance. Professional rugby can be very cut-throat and his role is crucial in helping players be organised off the field so they're not always reliant on, or worrying about, selection in a squad each year. Steve asked what I wanted from my career, how I wanted to portray myself, and he could see that I could develop a brand and put foundations in place around investing and managing money wisely, which is an area a lot of young players are uncertain about. Our relationship was more than professional and he has become a great friend; Steve was a sounding board, the warmest, friendliest guy around, and always had my best interests at heart.

Steve was also the person who made me aware of the social and personal responsibility that came with being a professional rugby player. Wellington is such a diverse and culturally lively place I could largely go unnoticed out on the streets early in my career, but in Taranaki or when we would travel to real rugby heartland areas I would be recognised more often. I've always known what it's like to be a kid who looked up to a rugby player, an idol; it's just that that player also happened to be my dad. I've tried to keep that in mind when I'm out and about and hope I've always remembered the value of a smile, wave or hello.

That awareness also transferred over to my own personal friendships. The first three years going from school to Taranaki, the Hurricanes and then the All Blacks were such a whirlwind and I may have lost connection with some of my mates. I was so focused and consumed by what I was trying to achieve and wanting to succeed that it was harder to maintain some friendships, and as things progressed I was also becoming more wary. My old friends, the ones from school who'd known me for years, provided the friendships I really came to value as there were more than a few people who I met along the way that tried to jump on the bandwagon. When there were offers and opportunities being thrown at me, I sometimes found out too late who wanted to be friends with me for who I was as a person, as opposed to who I was as a rugby player and what came with that. I knew in the back of my mind I had to be careful and have a wee bit of a guard up.

As time has gone on, everyone involved in rugby has learned much more about the mental side of the game both in terms of the importance of looking after our mental health and in preparing our brains as well as we prepare our bodies to play. Formal 'mental skills' practice or sports psychology isn't for everyone, but many of us will be utilising parts of it in our daily lives at school or work, such as planning and goal-setting, without even realising how much benefit we're getting.

Initially, I wasn't very big on goal-setting, mainly because in my mind I had no real right to be a Hurricane or an All Black — I was just a kid off a dairy farm. I had targets for all the physical things like body weight or how much I could bench press or squat, but when it came to setting goals for where I wanted to go in the game and what sort of career I could have, it was hard to understand how to even go about outlining those to myself or others.

I did know that I was excited to show that a skinny kid from the Naki could make it that far and perhaps inspire kids from rural New Zealand who don't necessarily go to the biggest schools or get all the opportunities. It wasn't until many years into my professional career that I learned how to translate something like that hope of being an inspiration into actual goals. In my first year as an All Black, that all went straight over my head and it wasn't until I spent more time with Gilbert Enoka that I came to understand it and see how it could be the difference between being good or being the best.

So much of it comes down to having good habits as early as possible. I definitely didn't realise it at the time, because it was all about fun, that even sketching out moves and planning out little ideas when I should have been studying in class was where I started some of my habits. Just like keeping the same goal-kicking routine, consistent effort in training, eating, rehab from injuries and other areas of the game are part of the

With Gilbert Enoka . . . he taught me the difference between being good and being the best.

steps to help a player improve regardless of what level they play at. When I was starting out, I could never have known how long my rugby career would last or if I would still be doing it 10 years later, but learning to be disciplined in my own planning and preparation has been a big factor in what I've achieved. Rugby was and should be so much about enjoyment, so I never put pressure on myself as a young player to get these things right every single time, but over the years I've found that being genuine in my prep, not cutting corners or taking a 'once over lightly' attitude has stood me in good stead.

Whenever times have been tough, I've gone back to remembering how much I always loved just simply playing rugby, kicking a ball in the backyard or crafting my Coke-bottle tee. If push came to shove and I wasn't enjoying the pressures of professional rugby, I could always go back to New Plymouth and play for Coastal with my mates on Saturdays.

Whenever times are tough, I always remember how much I simply enjoy playing the game.

But that would come with the compromise of working for a regular income instead of what rugby has given me: travel, the ability to make a living and set myself and my family up for the future, and some great friendships.

There can be a lot of scrutiny, and learning to deal with that has been a steep curve. Every so often, particularly early on, some of the criticism did give me a few doubts and negative thoughts, which is why I eventually chose not to read media coverage of the game. That actually wasn't easy for me because I've always been a total codehead, an avid follower and lover of rugby, and if I'm not playing I'll be watching the other Super Rugby teams to see how my mates are going. But I had to make the choice to pull back from reading or listening to the critiques quite early on, and I'm content with that. It could have consumed me otherwise.

I love being able to connect with people on social media, but it does have some negativity as well. There's simply no place for cyber-bullying and if you wouldn't say something to a person's face, why think you can do it online? There's no secret answer to how I deal with the bad side of it, although from time to time if someone is misinformed I'll reply with a simple fact or a smile . . . sometimes it may just be that I have to use the block button! Other than not going online at all, there's no way unfortunately to get rid of the bad stuff on social media entirely, but I try to be really positive about what I project and hope that others get enjoyment from it, only taking on board the opinions or advice of people I trust and respect.

There are many reasons why I play the game and my 'why' has changed over the years. My passion to play for Taranaki, the Hurricanes and the All Blacks, and ultimately my love of rugby, is what drove me early on, as well as simply wanting to get better at each skill regardless of what level that would take me to. But I've reassessed and re-evaluated as my career has progressed, and had to go from being a young player who wasn't into setting goals to someone who needed to be very real and honest about what I wanted to achieve.

It takes a bit of guts and you have to allow yourself to be vulnerable and proudly say where you want to go in life or your career. For me it was 'I want to start for this team, be the best in New Zealand in my position and then the best in the world in my position' . . . and then from there, woah, 'I want to be the best player in the world full stop' or even 'the best ever'. They're all very bold things to say.

I hopefully still have years ahead, but ultimately I'd like to be seen as a player who entertains the fans and is exciting to watch, that I play with pride for every team. I'd be happy just to show that it doesn't matter whether you're from a small, rural area or the big smoke and a big school, if you aim high in whatever you do and put in the hard work, you can achieve even the loftiest goals.

OPPOSITE: Aim high, do the work and you can achieve the biggest goals.

GETTY IMAGES

Family and friends at a Christmas barbecue, 2017.

ROB TUCKER

AFL
Tasmania

Autographs